The Backbone of Britain:
The people behind the craft

Written by Chris Roberts
Photography by Rob Evans
Design by Chris Roberts
Production by Chris and Rob
Editorial Advisor: Robbie Scott
Publisher: Fiona Shaw

Printed and bound in Leeds, UK by Team Impression.

ISBN: 978-0-9930221-8-0

A CIP catalogue record for this book is available from the British Library.

First published in June 2016 by Wordscapes
Wordscapes Ltd.
Second Floor, Elevator Studios
27 Parliament Street
Liverpool
L8 5RN
www.wordscape.org.uk

www.withloveproject.co.uk

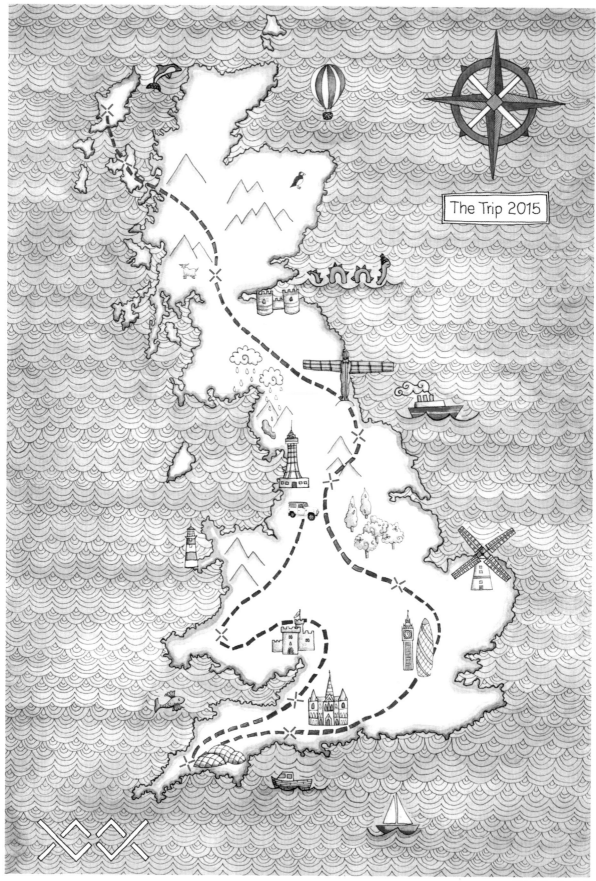

The Trip 2015

Map by Caroline Daly

CONTENTS

—

The people behind the craft

WELCOME
WITH LOVE PROJECT

—

www.withloveproject.co.uk

There was a slight drizzle in the air as I walked over to the Northern Quarter in Manchester to meet Rob. Quite normal weather for that time of year and certainly quite normal for Manchester. We met in a pub, parked ourselves on a wooden bench and drank a delicious but slightly overpriced ale and discussed the potential for a project.

I'm an art director and Rob's a photographer. Back in 2014 we decided to collaborate on a small project. We settled on visiting five people who produce things in this country, asking one question along the way... "Why do you do what you do?"

At the end of the five visits, the plan was to create a booklet which contained interviews and photographs of the people we met. Hiut Denim was our first stop. So very early one Friday morning we hopped in the car and headed to their open day in Cardigan, South Wales to meet a whole host of interesting individuals including cloth makers, potters, belt producers and more. They opened our eyes to a whole new world that we hadn't previously considered. So, on the journey back, we decided not to limit ourselves to just fashion, which was our original intention. Our focus was to now seek out 'people who produce things with a passion and a purpose'. This became our new mantra and it guided us on our travels, meeting people with extraordinary vision and talent.

We set up a blog immediately, that grew quickly. Every person we met led us onto someone new, another way of life, a new way of thinking. Everyone was extremely welcoming, passionate about their work and willing to talk us through the whole process. There aren't many projects which include a sign writer who has worked for the Kings of Leon next to a female blacksmith from Wiltshire, or a fair trade coffee roaster next to a couple glass blowing their way into numerous collections and national museums. We have met traditional furniture makers at the top of their game, motorcycle manufacturers hand building by eye, wheelwrights who can trace the family trade back to the 1300s and a tailor who produced suits for Pavarotti. Each one of these people has let us into their world after just a phone call or an email, understanding what we are trying to achieve and happy to share what they are producing.

The journey so far has given us the privilege of meeting over 30 truly inspiring individuals. We've been humbled by their openness, enthused by their work and empowered by their attitude. Some days we have driven round the corner to meet people, other days we've travelled for over 12 hours. Each journey is filled with the excitement of hearing another great story, an insight into someone's way of life and thinking. We really hope you enjoy the collection of stories we've gathered as much as we have enjoyed bringing them all together.

—

Chris and Rob

DONALD JOHN MACKAY

LUSKENTYRE HARRIS TWEED COMPANY

———

The wind whips up off of the green blue sea of Luskentyre and nips at our faces as we head to see Donald John Mackay, Harris Tweed maker. His weaving shed sits next to the house overlooking Luskentyre bay, one of the most beautiful beaches in Europe, where the sand is porcelain white and the water is a thousand shades of green and blue.

Donald has been weaving Harris Tweed here for over 45 years. Weaving goes back a long way in his family - both his father and grandmother made cloth and the process has hardly changed at all over the years. In order for the cloth to be called Harris Tweed, it has to be handwoven by islanders at their homes, finished and made from pure virgin wool dyed and spun all in the Outer Hebrides. From his shed behind the house, on a road by the sea, Donald has woven tweed for global brands, helping re-ignite the slowing Harris tweed industry. Back in 2011 he was awarded an MBE for his services to the industry.

We knock on the door and a loud Sottish accent belted out "come on in boys" from the back of the shed. We enter and see Donald stood, talking to someone. He looked over and says "I'll be with ya soon boys make yourself comfortable". The shed is split in two; we wait in the space directly below the loom, stacked rolls of Harris tweed igniting colour in the room and the sun shone in through a large window with an office view as special as they come. Looking out, it's

only the small road we drove up on that separates the house from flowing sand dunes, the beautiful beaches and the surrounding mountains rising from tropical-looking waters.

We wait patiently and have a good look around. Right next to the door and pinned to the wall is a print out of a range of Clarks Harris Tweed shoes. Donald had worked with the footwear brand to create tweed for the range. Clarks aren't the only household name Donald has worked for. Back in the '90s his wife Maureen, who he runs Luskentyre Harris Tweed with, took a call from Nike. They asked for some samples to try out in a new trainer. After sending off the samples Donald forgot about the phone call – that was until he said "They called back and wanted to order 10,000 yards of cloth for a trainer. I only weave on average 27 yards a day, so it would have taken me years to produce." But an order that size from a global giant like Nike isn't something you let slip. Donald set about mobilising weavers throughout the Outer Hebrides. Three months and lots of man hours later they had completed the order. Nike were delighted, the new Terminator trainer was a huge success and they rang back for another 10,000 yards.

Before the Nike order there were only around 80 weavers left in the Outer Hebrides, but the success of the Nike range raised the popularity of Harris Tweed exponentially, opening it up to a completely new audience and making

tweed 'cool' again. There are now over 200 weavers, producing cloth for everything from tailored suits to cushion covers. Donald says "Thankfully there is a new generation of weavers coming through, I've got nephews who weave and I'm delighted to be able pass on skills I learned from my father." This young blood coming through and a renewed global interest in the islands' handwoven cloth means the future of the Harris Tweed industry looks solid and incredibly bright.

"Nike called back and wanted to order 10,000 yards of cloth for a trainer. I only weave on average 27 yards a day, so it would have taken me years to produce."

———

KENNY MACLEAN
ISLE OF HARRIS DISTILLERS

———

www.harrisdistillery.com

After a full breakfast from the Calmac ferry canteen, we went up on deck to witness a double rainbow straight out of a Lucky Charms advert. The clouds parted and the sun burst through. It felt as though Harris was welcoming us in. As the ferry came into the head of the harbour in Tarbert, we could see the black and white church-like building that we would be visiting... the newly-opened Harris Distillery. We were meeting Kenny MacLean, Harris born and bred, currently working as the Project Manager for the distillery.

"We call ourselves the Social Distillery,"

—

Kenny grew up in Strond, a little village on the south coast of Harris, in a crofting community. He spent a number of years working in England but always knew he would come home to work. He is now in charge of spirit production and getting the distillery producing and selling the finest grade whisky and was keen to show us the process involved. All of the equipment (bar the charred whisky barrels) is brand new. The copper stills distilling the whisky burst through the second floor, rising up from a bowl-shaped bottom to a tight neck reaching high up to the roof. To the right of them, wooden washbacks where the fermentation took place. The entire room feels like a giant science experiment.

Downstairs is the nuts and bolts of the operation. The bottom of the huge stills dominate the space and stainless steel pipes shoot off left and right. Everything is meticulously clean. In an adjacent building we pull apart two huge wooden doors and peer into a room that has the whisky barrels in, hundreds of wooden barrels lay on their side with the "H" branding stamped on. Unfortunately we can't take any photos because Kenny says that "alcohol vapours seep out and the whole room is highly explosive, so you can't operate any electrical equipment here."

The chairman of the company Anderson Bakewell had been talking about setting up the distillery for seven years. He wanted to create something that would last for a long time and is determined to leave a legacy to Harris of employment, opportunity and confidence. To do that he has brought in top professionals within the industry, to make sure everything from taste right to distribution is the best it can be. Kenny says, "the people of Harris were very excited about the build. It was a bit like a soap opera, watching day by day the distillery come to life." They are now fully operational but, as Kenny says, "great things take time, we can't sell the first batch of whisky until 2020." What they are producing and selling right now is a top grade gin, infused with local, hand-harvested sugar kelp for a subtle sweetness. We were invited to have a taste and if the gin is anything to go by, then the whisky will definitely be worth the wait.

There aren't many businesses that can wait four or five years for a return, but then there aren't many businesses whose ethos revolves around the local community. "We call ourselves the Social Distillery," Kenny says. The opportunity for local people to get involved in a project so close to home, supporting and helping the Harris economy, has been irresistible to islanders. It's a fantastic story and hopefully in four years time it'll be a fantastic product. This business is built on solid foundations and supported by the community. The whisky may be a slow burner, but, as they say, good things come to those who wait. Slainte.

ROGER AND ANDREA HOLDEN
SKYE WEAVERS

—

www.skyeweavers.co.uk

It was rush hour on Skye as we set off at 08:30. Ten miles and 20 minutes later we had passed one man on a bike and a lady walking her dog. It's the kind of rush hour we wished faced us on a daily basis.

After meeting Roger on Mull, Andrea's holiday turned into more of a permanent stay. A while later they purchased a pedal-powered loom and housed it in a shipping container, before moving to a bothy with no electricity, about 20 minutes' walk up the hill. It was here they started working part time producing woven products. Andrea said "the wind would howl through the walls, it was very exposed but the scenery was amazing". They were both very new to weaving but got help from Bob Ryan, who set up the original Isle of Mull Weavers. Roger says "he's been fantastically supportive and helped us get up to speed". They honed their skills and got used to the pedal-powered loom on Mull, but wanted to make it a full time career and made the move to Skye. They set up business in the crofters cottage that Roger's family had bought as a holiday home back in the '60s.

The business took off from the moment they arrived; the loom is housed in a purpose-built wooden shed and next door lives their rather ingenious hand-built warping mill. It was built by Roger and Bob on Mull, tested and then flat-packed ready for the move to Skye. It now lives in a traditional stone outbuilding with original exposed beams. It's an impressive wooden and metal structure which rotates to collect a huge number of threads shooting off in all directions and neatly wraps them ready for weaving.

The sign for Skye Weavers was visible from the road; we turned into the driveway set high above the house and headed down the steep incline to meet a fantastic couple building a business powered by pedal. Roger and Andrea have set up shop in the outbuildings of their crofters cottage in Glendale, north west Skye. Everything they produce is woven on a pedal-powered loom, an environmentally sound and sustainable process.

Roger's background is farming and agriculture and it was on an organic farm on the Isle of Mull where two very important things happened. The first was meeting Andrea, who was cycling through Mull on holiday, and the second was working next to a weaving mill, which opened his eyes to this whole new world.

Arranged in another building is a selection of finished scarfs, tweed blankets, throws, shawls, wraps and more. The products are soft to touch and, as you would expect, contained beautifully hand-woven patterns. Andrea is the self-confessed creative of the two, using the surrounding landscapes and macro photography to influence her designs. Roger is the problem solver, the logical thinker bringing a beautiful symmetry to their work to produce items on the bike-powered loom, that are not only ethically and sustainably sound, but look and feel great as well.

It was pedal power that brought Andrea to Mull and it's pedal power that is now responsible for a future for the both of them and – judging by the products they produce and the interest in their way of life – that future is very bright.

COLIN CAMPBELL

MCROSTIE LEATHER

www.mcrostie.co.uk

the products McRostie produced for the equine industries. But it wasn't until a fashion shop in Glasgow asked Colin to produce belts for jeans that a new market opened up for them.

The space is open and clearly split into working areas. Various tools and cutting equipment sit proudly on a work surface illuminated by the large window in front of us. Directly behind that, in the centre of the room, is a table that holds a mountain of leather strips and off cuts. The walls are filled from floor to ceiling with small drawers, shelves and boxes containing items from specific tooling to various metal fixings. There are horse saddles, stirrups and harnesses, some hanging like trophy pieces and others waiting to be repaired, all hints of an equine past dating back to 1887.

After a fish supper, Irn Bru and a Tunnocks Tea Cake we head out of the centre of Glasgow to meet a heavyweight leather specialist. It is a short drive out into the surrounding green countryside where we meet Colin Campbell, the owner and director of McRostie Scotland. The company uses the finest British materials and traditional techniques to produce quality handmade leather products.

McRostie's was traditionally a master saddlers and harness makers, Colin took over in the 1980s and started to learn the ropes from Hugh Mason, master saddler, who had worked with leather all his life. He quickly learned the skills needed to make and repair

The focus now for McRostie is less on the equine industry and more in the fashion markets. They now produce products including belts, bags, document holders, kilt belts, sporrans and corporate gifts. However their most popular and best-selling belt owes its success to a horse harness Colin used as inspiration for the design. He says " I love to see products through from the initial design stage right through to the hands-on making, you just have to look around this place, there is inspiration everywhere." Their handmade, small run nature means they do occasionally get some strange requests. For example, Colin told us about a travelling circus which came

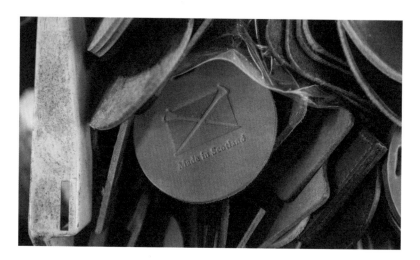

to Scotland. "The circus elephant had a sore foot and they asked if we could make a leather boot for him, which we duly did! It fitted perfectly.

More recently was the client who came in with a pair of green wellies and asked if I could transform them into a pair of 'Big Banana Feet' for a Billy Connolly tribute act he did. This was more of a challenge, but I think The Big Yin, as he is known in Scotland, himself would have been happy to wear them!"

Everything is produced in the workshop using the best British materials and now sells throughout the UK, Europe and in Japan, where the demand for handmade Scottish goods is very high. The handmade quality of each heavyweight piece is unique and the great thing about each item is that the use of full grain, vegetable-tanned bridle leather means they will only improve with age and wear.

JENNIFER KENT
EDITION SCOTLAND

—

www.editionscotland.com

We sip our flat white and Americano
at the pop-up café in the Southblock
Glasgow, as we wait for Jennifer Kent
of Edition Scotland. The space was
clean; white walls and high ceilings
punctuated with different pieces of
art hung around the room.

She takes us to her studio, a space dominated by bursts of vibrant colours radiating from yarn bundles, hanging cashmere scarves and design drawings scattered around. This is certainly a working environment, with plenty of energy.

Jennifer runs Edition Scotland, a company specialising in cashmere and merino scarves, as well as other accessories for men. She graduated from Glasgow School of Art with a First Class degree in Textile Design and a Masters with Distinction in Textiles as Fashion. Following a successful internship in New York and work at Lyle and Scott in London, she returned to Glasgow to launch Edition Scotland. While she was with Lyle and Scott, Jennifer had the chance to work with Comme des Garçons, giving her the opportunity to experience UK manufacturing at its best. She worked with Lyle and Scott factories in the Scottish Borders and it was here that she got the taste for hands-on manufacturing and knew it was something she wanted to do more of. The seed for Edition Scotland was sown.

"I love being back in Glasgow," she says, "there is definitely a community here – not just in this building but in the city itself." She had already made some great contacts with factories in the Scottish Borders and knew she wanted to work specifically with cashmere. The raw fibre for her scarves comes from a unique herd of cashmere goats in the Alashan region of Inner Mongolia. Each spring the precious fleece is hand-sorted and combed by nomadic herders before being transported to the mill on the banks of Loch Leven in Scotland, where it is dyed and spun into yarn. She says "the quality of the hand-sorted fleece, the skills of the cashmere mill in the Borders and the soft Scottish water all align to provide us with a beautifully soft product."

The scarves are so soft that once on you won't want to take them off. They are elegantly presented on bespoke hangers, and allow us to experience the unique softness and to admire the classic designs, which change every season. Jennifer says, "I'm really passionate about all of my designs having a depth to them and a story to tell. I take time to work on research and development because there is no way I just want to produce pretty patterns." The current designs are a blend of geometric abstract art fused with classic or fast-disappearing Scottish patterns.

Jennifer's scarves sell all over the world, with stockists in Japan and America as well as the UK. A lot of time goes into perfecting the designs, from carefully selecting the highest quality goat hair to the time-honoured manufacturing techniques used to produce each scarf - it's easy to see why Edition Scotland scarves are stocked in some of the finest stores worldwide.

"The quality of the hand-sorted fleece; the skills of the cashmere mill in the Borders and the soft Scottish water all align to provide us with a beautifully soft product."

———

ALEC FARMER
TRAKKE BAGS

———

www.trakke.co.uk

We pass a man moving band equipment to one side in a dark corridor as we board a service elevator. The door clunks shut and we hit number one. The lift rises slowly as we head to meet Alec from Trakke.

Trakke is a Glasgow-based outdoor lifestyle brand, producing kit you can wear in the city and also when you go to the hills. It was set up by Alec while he was studying graphic design at Glasgow School of Art and at weekends he would raid through skips to find whatever materials he could get his hands on, from old prams to abandoned suitcases and everything in between.

Then he'd cut his findings apart and start to make products out of them on his "old crappy domestic sewing machine". It wasn't long before he settled on making cycling bags. Alec started to sell these bags on a market in the east end of Glasgow and soon sold nearly 250 handmade individual bags. "I thought 'if I'm going to do this properly I want to do it to the best of my ability,'" he says. He knew that raiding skips wasn't exactly a career move so he broadened his approach and set about forging strong relationships with great British manufacturing companies, some of whom have been around for close on 200 years.

Trakke now works out of a building in the city and occupies a large space neatly split up into specific sections. As we enter the room to our left we are met with a fantastic array of colours from the latest selection of Trakke bags, some hanging and others neatly placed on a bespoke shelving system. On our right, Alec is separated from us by a floor-to-ceiling glass wall. He sits at the computer engrossed in his work, but Madeleine Wilson, studio assistant at Trakke greets us and gives us a quick tour. Just past the office entrance the space opens up and in front of us are a number of classic Singer sewing machines; neatly placed in the corner is the Trakke yurt, standing proud. As we round the corner there are a selection of

"I thought, 'If I'm going to do this properly, I want to do it to the best of my ability'"

fabrics neatly rolled, a shelf with easily accessible green drawers and two people busy making the bags from a list of orders.

Alec joins us and we head over to a piece of fabric we'd noticed earlier... it is dark blue and feels pretty tough. Alec unrolls it; tells us about the fabric which is wax cotton, looks beautiful, ages well and is very durable. "It was originally invented in Scotland by fishermen, so it has a great history forged in this country, as indeed does the Harris Tweed that we use, which is woven by pedal in the weavers' homes, shipped to the workshop and turned into bags for cycling."

The bags have great versatility and you can get a lot of use out of them. As well as using the best materials available they are individually made by a small passionate team. When a bag is being cut, Trakke sends the customer a photo and then another when it is being assembled, keeping them in the loop at all times about the production and giving them an insight into the workshop. Alec says "It's great when customers get back in touch and we see our bags well travelled. We got a photo from a girl who bought one of our weekend bags and took it around South America for six months".

Each bag is unique. It is individually made by professionals who take a pride in what they do. They are built to last and the materials look even better with age, seeming to fit to the person like a good pair of jeans. Every scuff, every mark helps build up a unique pattern of the owner and their adventures. As we left we knew it wouldn't be long before we had a Trakke bag on our backs.

JAMIE BARTLETT AND LUCY ROSS

BANTON FRAMEWORKS

———

www.bantonframeworks.co.uk

Just outside Glasgow we head down a single track road by a loch to meet Jamie Bartlett and Lucy Ross, founders of Banton Frame Works. Together they produce simple, contemporary eyewear made here in the UK.

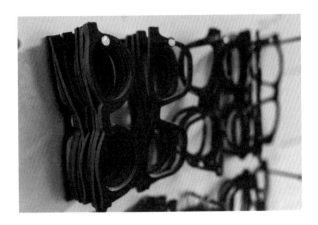

Their name comes from Banton Loch, situated right next to their workshop studio. The space is a large converted shed, neatly laid out with a mixture of purpose-built and bought-in equipment to handle the majority of their in-house processes; processes they have been refining since the couple met at university. It was Lucy who started to make glasses in her fourth year for her final major project and she enlisted Jamie's help as they were on the same product design course. They worked well as a team, and decided to set themselves a goal of showing and selling the glasses at Design Junction, a yearly trade show in London three months later. At this point they hadn't actually made and finished a pair, but as Lucy says, "it seemed so simple at the time. It was just a frame front, two sides and a hinge." Three very busy months later they were still finishing off the frames in the car on the way to London, but the show went well and they ploughed the money they made straight back into buying equipment.

From that point on the business grew organically. The pair continued adapting the process, improving, finding new ways to do things to a point they were happy with. There are now seven styles to chose from. Lucy says, "simplifying the collection of designs, materials and finishes allows us to really focus on getting the frames perfect." The designs themselves are classic and contemporary, with the synonymous riveted hinges that add that certain charm.

"It seemed so simple at the time...
It was just a frame front,
two sides and a hinge."

———

They are clearly passionate about making locally and are currently only one of a handful of frame makers here in the UK. Jamie says, "we are driven by material, process and design but more importantly what is achievable in this country." They have worked passionately to get to where they are now and have a process they are happy with, producing frames that are getting more and more popular, not just because of the design but also because of their ethos and values.

Simplifying their supply chain and bringing the majority of processes in-house has allowed the pair to build a business with solid foundations and, more importantly, made the manufacture of their eyewear far more sustainable and future proof. Jamie is already talking about apprenticeships and helping change the way eyewear is made in this country forever. Their enthusiasm and focus on getting the job done here in the UK is infectious and the processes they have in place are very scalable. They may be a small business now but they have big plans and a bright future.

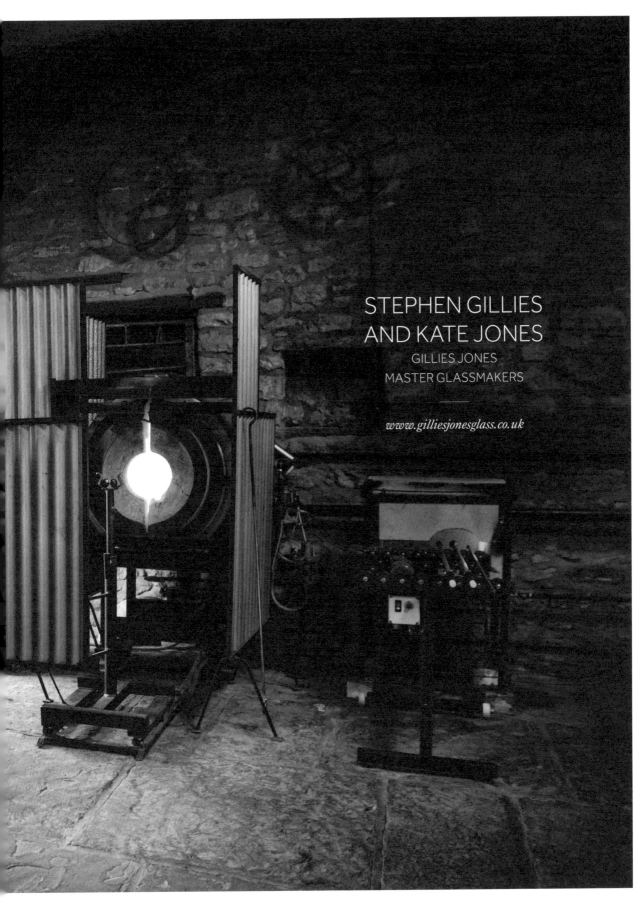

STEPHEN GILLIES
AND KATE JONES
GILLIES JONES
MASTER GLASSMAKERS

www.gilliesjonesglass.co.uk

We head for North Yorkshire, the sun beaming down and illuminating our way into this beautiful part of the country. We pass ploughed fields and glistening lakes on our way to meet glass artists Stephen Gillies and Kate Jones. They create visually stunning handmade glass in the picturesque village of Rosedale Abbey, North Yorkshire.

We pull up on the grass opposite; the door is open and we can see straight into the studio; a single storey converted barn. There are a number of pieces displayed in the gallery space, all with stunning colours and delicate designs. This unique art hits your eyes and the heat from the studio washes over you, radiating from the various kilns that stay fired for 11 months of the year. The space opens out to a large studio area where Stephen blows the glass. The warm room is very calming, everything has its own place, fitting the methodical processes of glass blowing.

Stephen and Kate have been producing glass blown pieces together in the traditional way for over 20 years. They both attended Stourbridge College of Art. However they only met after they'd finished their respective courses, which were in different parts of the campus. Kate trained as a painter while Stephen studied glass blowing. In time, Kate became fascinated by the world of glass and enrolled on a one year post grad course to learn all the practical skills and how to make the marks on glass that she'd previously made on paper.

Stephen continued to study the intricate art of glass blowing at various small studios around the world. He travelled to Denmark, Switzerland, the east coast of the United States as well as the Isle of White. Whenever Kate had the opportunity, she would fly out and assist Stephen and they soon realised they worked brilliantly together in work as well as life.

They opened their studio on May 1st 1995. Their style of working together is something they call 'creative bickering'. Stephen begins the process by blowing the glass and adding colour, before Kate creates her own imaginative patterns. Watching Stephen work and effortlessly move from one station to another is like watching a dancer execute carefully rehearsed dance steps. The processes, skills and tools involved in glass blowing haven't changed much since medieval times. He says "I love the simplicity of what I do, heating the glass so it is malleable and then when it's hot enough I have this small window of time before it cools again to get my shaping right. It's really exciting."

Once shaped, the glass then goes to Kate's space which is in another building adjacent to the barn. It seems busier than Stephen's. She calls it her 'creative chaos'. Stephen can blow the glass a lot faster than Kate can finish the pieces, so there are lots of them dotted around the room, some that are waiting to be worked on, some finished and some awaiting delivery. Kate smiles when she says "I love the space exactly like this, I know where everything is." She works on the blown glass, removing the top layer to create the patterns inspired by their rural location. "Living in this part of the world definitely influences my work, from the smallest flower to the rolling landscapes and the seasonal colours, I can't help but take it all in."

We were lucky enough to see the methodical glass blowing process for ourselves, which is an art-form in itself and understand the thinking and techniques behind Kates surface design. The two processes combine to produce decorative glass work which has received global recognition and it is easy to see why.... the confident use of colour and the marriage of shape and surface design make each piece a unique work of art.

"I love the space exactly like this, I know where everything is."

———

DAVID BEATTIE AND TRACY LEE
ROUNTON COFFEE ROASTERS

———

www.rountoncoffee.co.uk

The trusty sat nav dropped us in the general vicinity of Rounton Coffee Roasters, but we had to rely on our keen sense of smell to locate the barn. Fortunately for us David Beattie and Tracy Lee, owners of Rounton Coffee, were just finishing off a roast and the smell of fresh coffee wafted in through our air con. A quick U-turn and we followed our noses back to the barn door.

*"It all became clear. I knew
working with coffee was where
I wanted to be."*

———

Set in an old granary just outside Middlesbrough, in a small village called East Rounton, Rounton Coffee Roasters has been producing fantastic coffee since 2014. The old barn is full of character, exposed beams and original wooden floor, handmade wooden furniture, hessian coffee sacks and, of course, lots of shiny coffee equipment. David and Tracy had set up a cupping tasting session, guiding us through the subtleties of their unique blends and carefully chosen single origin coffees. We try six or seven different coffees, each one bringing its own taste and aroma, expertly guided by David whose knowledge and passion for coffee came through in abundance.

David started out in chemical engineering, so with a strong background in science you could say he is now the Walter White of the coffee world, but he didn't set out to roast. Back in 2011 he left his engineering job to travel the world. He remembers... "I finished on Thursday and on Friday I jumped on a train at Middlesbrough train station and headed to France, then around Europe, into Russia, down to Mongolia, China and ended up in Lake Toba, Sumatra."

He went deep into the Sumatran forest and spent time with coffee farmers in a small co-operative. He was hooked instantly, wanting to learn all about the process. He says, "it was here where it all became clear. I knew working with coffee was where I wanted to be." After initially trying to set up sustainable trade routes to the UK while in Sumatra, he realised the best thing he could do was to set up his own market, so he headed home with a plan to start roasting.

When he arrived back he met up with Tracy, now his partner, who he had known since school. They went for a coffee. Tracy says, "David was so excited and passionate about setting up a roastery, and then, hopefully, coffee shops, that I couldn't help but get involved." Eighteen months later the business was launched from the granary, and has

grown and grown. David says, "every day we are learning, improving and strengthening everything we do." The idea from the start was to bring consistent quality coffee back to his home town of Middlesbrough and do it on a sustainable basis, guaranteeing a fair cut for everyone at the bean end, and a fabulous taste for everyone at the cup end.

So far they have won taste awards, run numerous public cupping sessions, are stocked and served throughout the UK and have finally opened their first coffee shop in Middlesbrough town centre. The great tasting coffee, the solid roasting process and David's relentless drive all add up to a recipe for success and his vision of serving great tasting coffee consistently, whilst giving farmers a fair cut, is starting to happen. And with plans for more coffee shops, it won't be long before Rounton coffee becomes one of the solid names in the coffee world. We'll drink to that.

NATALIE STAPLETON
MCNAIR MOUNTAIN SHIRTS

———

www.mcnairshirts.com

We headed to Huddersfield, the heart of the
UK's woollen textile industry to meet Natalie
Stapleton at McNair. With a talented team
and a traditional and principled approach to
manufacturing in Britain, McNair are busy
producing the best mountain shirt in the world.

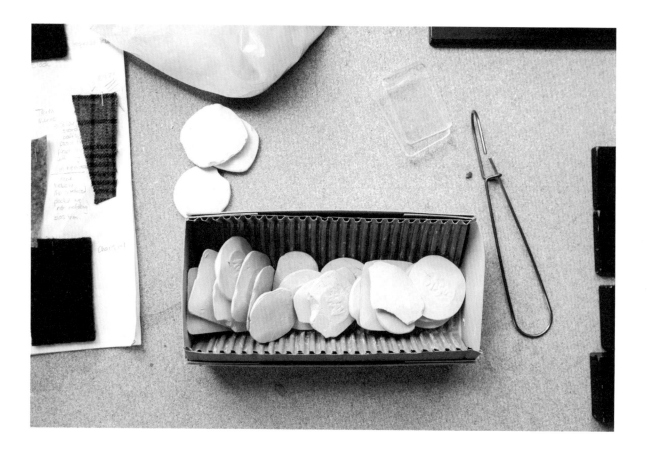

Up a few flights of solid stone stairs we enter into the space that McNair occupy on the third floor of this traditional Yorkshire Mill. The whole floor is open plan, light floods in from the large windows which occupy all four walls and bounces off the varnished original wooden floorboards below our feet. The whitewashed brick walls are broken up with a half height blue paint and various styles and colours of shirts hang dotted around the space. As Natalie shows us around, the team are busy in production, cutting, stitching, ironing and carefully, piece by piece, assembling the world's best Merino mountain shirt. Natalie told us "excluding any of the buttons there are over forty five separate pieces in each shirt." Every little detail has been considered and is carefully constructed by hand, then when finished is signed and numbered, this attention to detail is so important in everything they produce. Natalie says "When we set out to make the shirt we didn't start with a price point and work backwards, we set out to make the best shirt we could and then worked out how much it would cost."

She has worked in textiles for over 20 years and has been in Huddersfield for just over ten, becoming more and more fascinated in the wool industry and its strong heritage in Huddersfield. Her background is in technical textiles and, whilst working for a performance fabric brand, she met Richard Hamshire, who – along with Neil McNair, a professional snowboarder – had started to work on the original McNair shirt. Natalie was hooked from the initial chat and quickly fell in love with the idea of producing an outdoor shirt made from wool, the original technical fabric. She mentions "Richard's inspiration for the shirt came from a pair of traditional Dachstein mitts he wore in the mountains." He already knew Neil McNair so had the perfect person to test and help develop the shirt. They wanted to create something that looked great and performed brilliantly and knew that couldn't be done quickly. The whole process of designing, prototyping, testing, re-developing and refining was about two years.

"When we set out to make the shirt we didn't start with a price point and work backwards, we set out to make the best shirt we could and then worked out how much it would cost"

The design is a collaboration of garment technologists, tailors, numerous mills and testers, combining to produce an enhanced Merino shirt which regulates temperature naturally and keeps you more comfortable in variable conditions for longer. The shirt is not only technologically and aesthetically brilliant but, as we look out of the third floor windows, Natalie points out in the direction of a number of other mills that help with the weaving, milling, raising and steaming of the shirt, which is all completed within ten miles. "Without the support and truly world-leading expertise of the local mills we would never have been able to create fabric as soft, strong, comfortable and protective as we have. It's a product that couldn't have been made anywhere else." The raw Merino wool does currently come in from Australia or Chile but McNair's ongoing development and prototyping with British breeds means that in the near future the shirt could be sourced and made right here in the UK.

They have only been selling to the public for just over two years but in that time they have received global acclaim. You only have to try one of the shirts on to instantly feel the quality and know that a purchase is on the cards. The fit, the style, detailing, the craftsmanship of every shirt all combine to make this product truly "the best mountain shirt in the world".

STUART MITCHELL
STUART MITCHELL KNIVES

—

www.stuartmitchellknives.com

Walking through the archway to Portland works, you instantly get a feeling that something is happening. Clanging, grinding, bashing sounds are ringing out from over 20 workshops housed in this historic building. A building that has held a wide variety of makers since the late 1800s and now is the last fully-working integrated steel works left standing in Sheffield.

This particular works is interwoven into Sheffield's industrial past, it was here, the first ever stainless steel knife was produced. A steel that was also found right here in Sheffield by Harry Brearley on 13th August 1913 whilst experimenting for a small arms manufacturer. Harry's employers weren't interested in the rust free steel at all, so he bought some from them and took it along to Portland Works, where he perfected the new steel.

Our visit to Stuart Mitchell knives is a visit to heart of the steel industry. The building where stainless steel was born and one which has held the Mitchell family for over 35 years, allowing them to craft some of the finest knives coming out of Sheffield.

Stuart's workshop is crammed full of character, with numerous machines that look as old as the building, shelving stacked full of metals and off cuts of steel leaning against the wall. All illuminated by the light bursting through the many single pained windows and sky lights.

Stuart welcomes us in and took us on a grand tour of his workshop and then the building, which is now a co-operative, bought and proudly owned by 500 shareholders including the current workers, people across the city and the rest of the world. He talks about the process of making the knives, the bespoke nature of what he does, the family history and his ideas for the future. It is clear to see he is proud of what he creates, taking up to three months to perfect every knife that goes out. Working through each process with care and precision, from the initial design and hand cutting to the forging, grinding and finishing.

Each knife is numbered, emphasising the bespoke nature of this craft and ensuring no two knives are the same. This individuality is something his customers love. Stuart encourages them to come to the workshop so together they can design the perfect knife, allowing customers to have a real connection with the product they are buying.

The quality and time taken to produce each knife attracts a lot of attention, meaning that if you want a knife from Stuart you will have to join a waiting list of eager clients. Ask anyone who owns a Stuart Mitchell knife and they will tell you it is definitely worth the wait.

JON CROMPTON
WALSH TRAINERS

—

www.normanwalshuk.com

On to Bolton to meet Jason and his father Jon Crompton who, with Jon's brother Dennis, now own Norman Walsh UK, the only 100% British made and owned sports shoe company.

He takes us into the factory, past a wall of trainer casts, a row of workers on Singer sewing machines and large cutting equipment punching out the various shapes needed for the perfect Norman Walsh trainer. Before we are taken to see the production of the trainer, Jason gives us a quick history of this inspirational company. He tells us that Bolton was, in fact, the birthplace of the running shoe. This iconic shoe was invented by J.W. Foster and Sons in 1898. Norman Walsh actually served his apprenticeship here after leaving school in 1945 at the age of 14. The Fosters soon recognised Norman's skills and he started to make their 'elite athletes' shoes. He eventually became a master craftsman making shoes for the 1948 British Olympic team, including Roger Bannister and later on Sir Chris Bonnington.

J.W. Foster and Sons became 'Reebok' in 1958 and, a few years later in 1961, Norman left the firm to set up on his own company, Norman Walsh UK, operating from the back of his parent's terraced house, where he made shoes for rugby, football, mountain climbing and cross country. In the early '70s he started to produce running shoes for the marathon boom and many of these shoes are still being produced to the same design and following the same traditional techniques today.

"That's it. No negotiation. No messing about. Take it or I close the factory"

—

After a lifetime in the trade Norman retired in 1996, selling the business to the Crompton family. All members of the family had grown up wearing Walsh trainers, buying them direct from the factory and getting to know Norman at the same time. They fell in love with the idea of owning the business and kept asking him if he wanted to sell. Norman was non-committal at first. Then one day, out of the blue, as Jon was buying yet another pair of training shoes, Norman quoted a figure to Jon and said, "That's it. No negotiation. No messing about. Take it or I close the factory." Jon says, "We tried to bring him down in price. No good. We agreed to pay the full 'whack' and Norman was pleased to sell to us. He was a bit of a cheeky so and so though because he said to us....'any chance of paying in cash?' We laughed, and shook hands and we were on our way. Brilliant."

Norman gladly acted as a consultant to the brothers for many years but sadly passed away in 2014. His legacy though lives on. The brothers have been studying Norman's back catalogue and slowly releasing some of his original designs, working closely with traditional suppliers to re-open old sole moulds and buying large quantities of suede from the same tannery in Scotland. As a result, many of the shoes being produced today are exactly the same as they were 40 years ago. We are lucky enough to see some of the original designs. There is a beautiful lime green running shoe from the '70s and the original track spikes he produced at Foster and Sons shortly after the Second World War. We were also treated to a sneak preview of the latest styles for next season. You would definitely be hard pushed to buy only one pair from this collection.

The demand for Norman Walsh shoes continue to rise, selling far beyond the UK to countries including America, Japan, Russia, Korea and they are now opening up a market in Chile. It is exciting times for this Bolton-based family company, and it is easy to see why more and more people appreciate what Norman Walsh UK is producing. As well as carefully sourcing the right materials, the factory still hand make every shoe. Every cut, every stitch is carefully watched over by the highly-trained staff, taking the process from pieces of fabric and rubber to the fully assembled trainers, producing high quality, cutting edge products with a fantastic heritage that can be worn by everyone.

JOHN ROGERS
LISSOM & MUSTER

———

www.lissomandmuster.com

A few steps down off Tib Lane and
you are in the world of Lissom and
Muster. A beautifully laid out store
full of products carefully chosen by
the owner, John Rogers.

"We think it's important to follow the ethos through in everything we do

---

A former social scientist and educationalist turned retailer, John believes in designing and sourcing skilfully made products fit for purpose. This belief takes him all over the country seeking out the mills, factories and practising makers who create these timeless items. This search is not only to ensure his store holds the finest pieces but also to fully understand the materials, processes and possibilities for their production. This allows him to let his customers know the quality and story behind each piece and ensures L&M houses some of the best-made pieces of clothing, footwear, accessories, print and homewares these islands have to offer.

One such collaboration with Cherchbi has seen a collection of beautifully crafted bags, leather goods and accessories, all produced featuring wool cloth from Cumbrian Herdwick sheep; leather tanned in Derbyshire; Cheshire brassware and a waterproof bonded cotton made in Oldham. It's these types of close collaborations that mean L&M can offer exclusive items with outstanding qualities.

Attention to detail is clear throughout the L&M experience – even the swing tags are uniquely produced with paper made in a mill in Cumbria; letter-pressed in Manchester; tied with twine made in Bolton and riveted and embossed in house. John says "We think it's important to follow the ethos through in everything we do – it seems a shame to dilute a locally-made product that we've put so much effort into, with a swing tag or packaging made on the other side of the world by people I'll never meet."

It is this attention to detail, combined with many years of hard work, that have helped to make this store what it is today. And it is easy to see why once people have found it, they keep coming back time and time again.

KEITH, KIT, GUY, LUKE, DAN, NATHAN AND GREG MCAVOY.
SEVEN BROTHERS BREWERY

———

www.sevenbro7hers.com

Setting up any business is tough, but setting up a business with seven family members is surely madness. Not for the Seven Brothers Brewery.

Walking into the warehouse it is plain to see this is a real family affair. We are greeted by Keith and quickly shown around, meeting brothers, wives and children. Anyone would have thought we were in Italy.

It was a momentous occasion, the first batch of Seven Brothers IPA being bottled as we arrived. It was a lovely atmosphere and a real sense of pride swept around the place as the bottles were filled. These bottles were ten months in the making, ten months of building, planning and brewing coming to fruition.

The seven brothers, Salford lads, have grown up showing entrepreneurial spirit from an early age and were all eager to work together at some point. But it wasn't until the second oldest brother Keith returned from a trip to Oslo that the chance to go into business appeared.

Like any good business idea, this one came about after a few pints, but unlike – many business ideas – this one actually involved a few pints. Seven to be precise, seven brews for seven brothers. Keith pitched the idea to the brothers in their local pub. Everyone was hooked instantly. From that moment forward the brothers have set about making their dream a reality, pouring all of their time and effort into the business. Learning and perfecting new skills. They will be producing a modest 4,000 bottles a week to start with, increasing month by month as demand grows. They are already in a number of Manchester's and the UK's finest bars and bottle shops, they supply a number of supermarkets and will soon be opening their own bar.

Making craft ales is nothing new, but there is something about Seven Brothers. It might be the solid business plan, the great tasting range of beers, or the fact this brewery is entirely family owned. Or maybe it's a little bit of all of these points that make this collection of entrepreneurial individuals so special and interesting. The early signs are pointing to a bright future ahead for the brothers, flying the flag for craft beers, Salford and true family spirit.

JOE HARTLEY
JOE HARTLEY

—

www.joehartley.org

Just beyond the Mancunian Way, past
Castlefield, where all the old buildings are
being re-purposed or knocked down to make
way for the ever-growing apartment lifestyle,
Joe Hartley and a number of other artists and
makers occupy a three storey building.

His shared space is neatly divided into three, a woodwork area, a ceramics area and a middle space dividing the two which is the office/garment area. The woodwork area is the space you enter into and it is full of activity, sawdust filling the room and the sound of cutting, sanding and shaping rings through the floor. We quickly move past the noise and through the office into Joe's ceramic space. The use of different mediums is obvious all around the room – as you enter you have to pass a set of stools, stacked in a row, the first is made out of coppiced hazel foraged from the space over the road, the slick looking stool next to it is made out of oak he found in the skip downstairs and the furthest on the right

is a set of stools he's designed for an upcoming pub, neatly stacked on top of each other. Just past the stools is a kiln with a few ceramic pieces scattered on top, and past that, an area with a bike leaning just below a huge wall mounted world map. This sets the tone for the rest of the space, an eclectic mix of objects and materials, tools and equipment.

Joe describes himself as, "Butcher, Baker, Designer, Maker – which sums up the cross discipline way I work." He is a product designer who works with wood, clay and cloth. The "Butcher and Baker" refers to Joe's time before university when he worked in more traditional jobs and it wasn't until he was 26 that he went to Manchester Metropolitan University and did a 3D Design degree. He graduated and left after winning the Business Design Centre's New Designer of the Year award 2012. That helped kick-start his career and his exhibition at the Craft Centre Manchester opened him up to the Manchester scene. Shortly after that he moved into the workshop he shares today, a mixed use building full of makers and artists.

Throughout his space there are lots of experimental pieces dotted around, each piece has its own story to tell. We found a wooden box that holds a shirt and then turns into a

hanger; a garment made out of an old Litchfield tent, utilising everything from the toggles to the guy ropes and a coffee cup that measures the exact amount of filter coffee needed. Each piece has a personality and playfulness of its own. Before his current project, 'the Pilcrow pub', everything he made was relatively small, using his bike to dictate the size... if it didn't fit in his panniers he didn't make it.

He is currently working as lead maker and facilitator of the Pilcrow pub. A pub, which is being built in Manchester by an army of volunteers. Joe's job is to facilitate the making of the pub through a variety of workshops. He says "With so many people involved, the prospect of group making is really exciting and it will be great to see what we will end up with." Although he doesn't make everything, Joe will be involved with everything that is made at the Pilcrow. Joe and a skilled team of volunteers with years of knowledge will help produce something that will become completely unique in its realisation and execution. Everyone is excited to see what will be produced, none more so than Joe, who is involved until September when the pub opens, but there are plans in place for the Pilcrow Legacy to continue so it can, as he put it "dovetail into the future".

The projects Joe has been involved with so far in his short career are as varied as his style of work. It is safe to say whatever the future brings, for Joe it will be a creative hive of activity fuelled by his curious nature and playful personality.

CHRIS HOLDEN
AJOTO

———

www.ajoto.com

The old Manchester mills are full of character. We love meeting people who have offices there. There always seems to be so much for your eyes to take in. We enter through a heavy steel door and approach the industrial elevator, close the meshed sliding door and creak slowly to the fourth floor where AJOTO is situated. Their space is great... original wooden flooring, high ceilings, exposed brickwork, steel and timber beams and all open plan. We are meeting Chris Holden, founder and owner of a company that produce beautiful tools for your journey.

Chris studied Design for Industry at Northumbria University. After he finished his course he went to London to work for a number of design and innovation consultants, using creative thinking to help businesses find new ways to connect with their customers. After a while he decided "if I'm doing this for large multi-nationals and start ups, then why can't I do this for myself?" So he decided to set up his own design consultancy, with a focus on working with ambitious small businesses. He also set himself a challenging and interesting task. Find a tool he uses every day, break it down, reinterpret it and make a new one within four weeks. The first tool he chose to re-design was a pen and that's where the story of AJOTO began.

After the four weeks he joined forces with Tim Higgins to progress the idea and then turned to Kickstarter to see if people would buy the product. They did and AJOTO smashed their original target figure in the process. Their journey began. "We wanted a brand that reflected our creative lifestyles. The pens were secondary to the intention though... our intention was to make something better than anyone else and then tell the story."

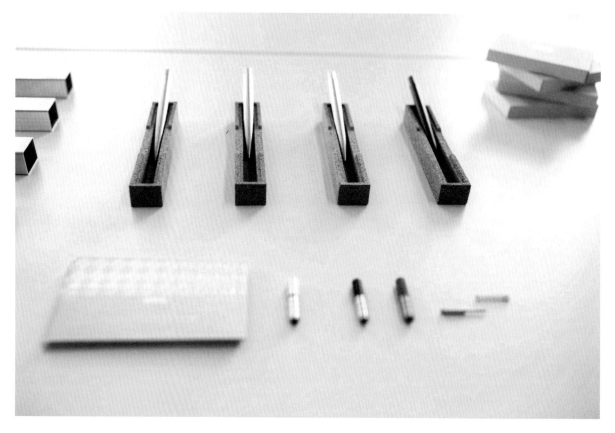

Chris says "We are constantly thinking of other products, but we don't make for making's sake. The first product we wanted to design was the product that we could use to design other things... hence the pen." It was this original tool that first attracted us to AJOTO. The minimalist design and simplicity of the pen is stunning, but it's the detail that is totally unique and compelling, containing seven key components that are precision machined by the finest manufacturers in the UK and Europe. The paper in their packaging is sourced from the highly regarded GF Smith paper merchants, produced by the world's best paper mill James Cropper in Cumbria and printed using traditional techniques by the specialist printers Identity in Tonbridge, Kent. As well as the obvious qualities there are also hidden details that reveal themselves through the patterns, symbols, unique markings and messages in both the packaging and the pen itself.

AJOTO's story is one which projects an open approach to educating the customer about every step of the manufacturing process and Chris' meticulous focus on detail elevates each piece to another level. In a world of mass production and invisible supply chains, the sustainable, open and honest approach AJOTO take is really refreshing.

DAVID JAYET-LARAFFE
FROG FLORAL ARTISTRY

—

www.frogflowers.co.uk

"If you have an idea in your head, if you want to create something you just have to go for it. Just do it."

———

Walking through the doors at Frog your eyes are hit with a visual treat... floral displays hang from the ceiling and rise from the floor, flooding the room with colour and style; framed neon lights radiate orange hues, floral wallpapers and framed prints sit proudly on the walls and a China tea set is waiting sat on the front desk, ready for our arrival.

David Jayet-Laraffe, owner of Frog pours the teas and tells us about how he started his floral artist studio. He moved to the UK from France 17 years ago, planning to stay in Manchester for a year or so, but he fell in love with the place and never left. While working as a waiter he started to experiment with floral design, saying "I would take the old flowers from the restaurant home and make my own displays." After seeing his displays, his friends encouraged him to think seriously about floristry, so he did; he went back to college and shortly after got a job for an international florist in Manchester and London. This gave him the skills and exposure he needed and it wasn't long before he knew exactly where he wanted to go and decided to open Frog, a floral artist studio, mixing his love for flowers, fashion and art. He is based in the creative hub of Manchester, the Northern Quarter. He says, "It's not just because it's trendy and I could grow a beard, but because I want to be surrounded by creative people and creative influences." Working with flowers allowed his natural creativity to flow and has seen him commissioned to design floral displays for hotels, restaurants, photoshoots, art installations as well as weddings and events.

"The majority of my work comes from word of mouth so it is important to have very good personal attention and care," he says. David works on an appointment-only service, allowing him to spend quality time with his clients. "In the first meeting with the client I don't give opinions, I just listen. I'm like a sponge. I take notes and get to know their requirements. It is my job to create a floral statement so I will do drawings, make notes, show flowers. It's this organic process growing between myself and the client that I truly love."

Every job is completely different but David makes sure everything that leaves his studio has his unique creative stamp of approval. "The best part is to see the initial ideas and the sketches come to life. It's so satisfying to have happy customers who love what we have produced together."

There are flashes of his creative personality all over the studio from the plastic flamingo striding out of a flower pot, to the porcelain rabbit sat next to a mannequin head with a leafy plant hairpiece. As he holds his golden gun mug he says, "If you have an idea in your head, if you want to create something you just have to go for it. Just do it." Spending time with David, it is easy to see why clients trust him to produce beautiful statement pieces. He oozes creativity and is instantly likeable, speaking passionately and painting pictures of the work he produces. It's obvious he lives and breathes what he does, taking inspiration through into his work. From simple statement pieces to flourishing floral displays, you can guarantee David will deliver unique pieces of work with a big red creative cherry on top.

PETER WILSON

BARTINGTON FORGE

—

www.bartingtonforgeblacksmith.co.uk

We arrive at Bartington Forge and peer into the workshop to see Peter Wilson hammering two molten pieces of metal together. We wait until the sparks have died down before introducing ourselves.

"As long as I'm stood next to my fire and anvil I'm happy. I just love making things and finding new engineering solutions with traditional blacksmith techniques."

———

Peter Wilson is a second generation blacksmith at Bartington Forge. He works from a beautiful setting, set back slightly from a canal, overlooking Cheshire's green fields. The building itself is steeped in history, dating back to the First World War when it was a coal dump. There are reminders dotted around about the age of the building, such as the air raid shelter sign which still sits on the wall at the front. Inside it's dark, but the natural light bursts through the open door and windows, and the warm orange glow rises from the forge like an early morning sunrise. There is a huge selection of tools, mostly handmade, hung up on the walls and a number of industrial machines that catch your eye, but the whole workshop centres around the forge and the classic blacksmith anvil. Peter says "They say the master of all trades is the stone mason but I would say it's the blacksmith. You have to have tools before you can make anything. We make the tools."

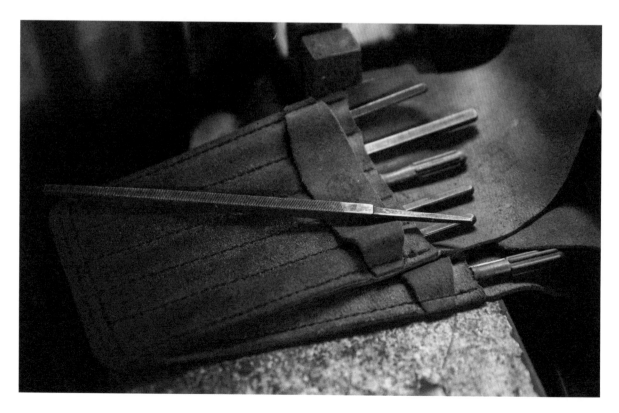

Peter's dad David, now retired, bought the place after leaving the army and set up the blacksmiths forge. Peter took over at the age of 22, but was tinkering away from the age of 11 in his dad's workshop. He has always been interested in producing things with his hands and it seemed only right to carry on the business. He now works on various types of blacksmithing, from traditional equipment repairs to bespoke pieces. We were introduced to Peter through Hugh Miller, a Liverpool based carpenter who had worked with him on a project with a church in Chester. Hugh handled the woodwork side of the job and Peter designed and made a metal cross with wheat detailing. Both were quality designs, finished to a highly professional degree. Peter works collaboratively on quite a lot of projects, but states that "as long as I'm stood next to my fire and anvil I'm happy. I just love making things and finding new engineering solutions with traditional blacksmith techniques."

With all the people we have met so far it is obvious to see that there is a huge satisfaction from producing things by hand. The whole process of blacksmithing... firing, melting, hammering, shaping and manipulating strong material into brilliant shapes and designs must take that achievement to another level. You would be hard pressed to find an occupation where you work in a darkened room, practically overheating; stand next to a fire all day; have to wear protective gear so you don't go blind or burn your skin; destroy any clothing you have and are covered in black metal dust, but feel completely satisfied with your day's work and smile as often as Peter does. His is a labour of love and it was a privilege to be there to witness it.

PHIL CHRISP
E.E. CHRISP LETTERPRESS

———

www.chrispprinters.co.uk

Based just south of Manchester, you would
be forgiven if you walked straight past E.E.
Chrisp Printers. Working out of a purpose-built
garage at the side of his house, Phil Chrisp
is responsible for a large percentage of all
letterpress printing coming out of
Manchester right now.

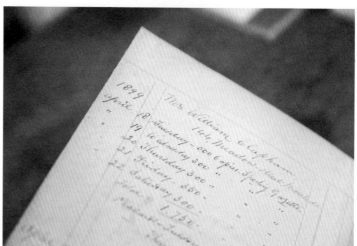

A printing process that nearly died out years ago, letterpress is making a resurgence today because of a uniquely tactile quality that designers and customers are enjoying once again. Back in the '60s litho printing completely changed the printing industry and letterpress machines were scrapped or given away, because the technique was no longer economically viable. Luckily, there were a few printing houses that held onto these beautiful machines and Phil's company was one of them.

E.E. Chrisp was founded back in the 1800s, Phil shows us his grandad's order book, with the first entry reading 1899. There are lots of gems like this in his workshop, giving a real sense of a family business and a lifetime's work dedicated to printing. Phil joined the business after college and was trained up on the letterpress machines, saying "back then you were taught to make a 'kiss' impression, so there was little or no impression when printing. These days it's the deep impression on thick stock that people love." Shortly after he entered the business the letterpress started to die out with the introduction of litho, but Phil held onto the Heidelberg platen, a machine that he still uses today. It moved with him to its new home out of the city centre, where it has enjoyed a new lease of life. "It's funny," he notes. "I saw the litho takings steadily overtake the letterpress before it became almost obsolete and now it's turned nearly full circle. Most of my output these days is letterpress."

When you look around the workshop it is clear to see that Phil is excited by the process and the work he produces. He keeps lots of examples which he happily showed us describing the types of inks, the papers and the impressions used. Each printed piece just as special as the next. That's the beauty with the letterpress, because of the nature of the printing each impression has tiny unique differences. It's the tactile nature of this printing, the tradition and hands on approach, the time taken for each job and the unique finished articles that all combine to see a real resurgence of this traditional printing method.

"Back then you were taught to make a 'kiss' impression. These days it's the deep impression on thick stock that people love."

BRITA HIRSCH
HIRSCH TAILORING

———

www.hirschtailoring.com

According to the UN World Tourism Organisation, the Silk Road begins in Xian, the ancient capital of China, and ends in the Cheshire town of Macclesfield, which is where we met Brita Hirsch, Bespoke Tailor, one sunny day in October. And, rather fittingly, it is Macclesfield silk which often lines her tailored suits.

Using the right materials is key to everything Brita does. When we first tried to meet her, she was visiting the Western Isles, sourcing Harris Tweed directly from weaver Donald John Mackay MBE, who famously helped the revival of the heritage cloth by securing a deal with US sports wear manufacturer Nike back in the '90s.

We eventually catch up with her at her Macclesfield studio, which has views across the hills of the Peak District and is perfectly placed for a trip to the famous Yorkshire woollen mills. Brita is a firm believer in sourcing materials from manufacturers who are within reach and points out that "I try to get to know all my suppliers personally; it is important for me to establish a trusting relationship, knowing that they are as passionate about what they produce as I am about what I create."

Her most important driver is to make the best possible garment for her customer. Be it a business suit, an outfit for a formal occasion or a classic tweed jacket, she will make sure it is just perfect. Having developed her passion for quality and precision during a three year traditional apprenticeship in Germany, in her first job she tailored costumes for the musical 'Phantom of the Opera' in Hamburg. "But it was during my time with master tailor Tom Reimer when my skills were really honed." His love of 1940s Italian and British style and insistence on using only the most meticulous hand sewing techniques meant she had opportunity to develop her craftsmanship to the highest level.

These skills were put to the test in the mid '90s when the late, great Luciano Pavarotti casually walked into the tailors, asking to be measured for a suit. He was keen to meet everyone involved and familiarise himself with materials, tools and techniques used. Brita says "it was clear that the man was genuinely interested in the craft – and in the people who delivered it." It was decided she would make a tailcoat in white silk and after, overcoming her initial awe, Brita got on with the work and made sure "this was best suit the man had ever worn."

As well as being a skilled tailor, Brita has qualified and worked as a textile engineer for years, developing highly technical fabrics for airbag production. Her engineering background allows her to look at her product from an investigative angle, feeding back into every bespoke piece she produces.

"It was during my time with master
tailor Tom Reimer when my skills
were really honed"

———

Her client base is global, with customers travelling from as far as the Hollywood Hills for a Hirsch tailored suit. The process takes her around 80 hours, from pattern draft to fitting to finishing touches. She would not dream of outsourcing any of her work, firmly believing in accountability that can only be assured through making entirely in-house. This level of skill and attention is seldom found away from the Savile Row tailors and importantly, it is even rarer to find a tailor who can produce the same quality for both a male and female fit. It is this knowledge and understanding of fabrics combined with her many years of practice that make her suits truly personal and unique pieces of craftsmanship.

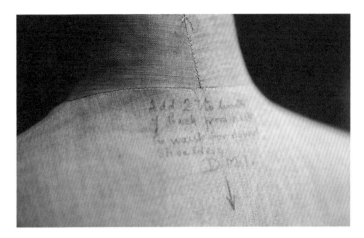

PAUL ROBINSHAW
FLOUR, WATER, SALT

———

www.flourwatersalt.co.uk

The smell of bread is enough to put a smile
on the face of most people. But that smell,
combined with the view of a 1979 Citroen
delivery van and a row of perfectly-formed sour
dough loaves, brought a grin from ear to ear.

Proud to be named after the ingredients they use, Flour Water Salt is a bakery borne out of a love and satisfaction for handmade bread. This love came about one day at a bread making course where Paul Robinshaw, a former high level IT specialist, baked his first batch of loaves. Although, in his words "the first loaves were all over the place," the satisfaction of having something he'd produced was immediate. He was hooked and set about learning as much as he could about artisan baking.

The first loaves were baked from his home oven, but word got out about these handmade loaves, using only the best organic ingredients and the business grew from strength to strength. Paul left IT to focus on baking and is now situated in Macclesfield, with a small family run team producing

"The first loaves I baked were all over the place"

bread slowly, the way it should be, without any additives or improvers. Each loaf takes a full day to produce, resulting in delicious bread that has more and more people in the North queuing up to sample.

Moving from a fast paced, high paid life in IT, to an artisan baker was a brave move to make, but one that has paid off completely. Speaking with Paul it is obvious to see he loves what he does and people love the bread – 'Flour, Water, Salt' produce. There is a great selection of breads now, all baked with the same care and attention, but, for us, the sourdough is king. In a world where life is speeding up and technology is taking over, there is something wonderful about the perfect simplicity of this slowly prepared loaf with its three ingredients that makes sourdough so special.

HUGH MILLER
HUGH MILLER FURNITURE

———

www.hughmillerfurniture.co.uk

"It's great to use the traditional way of bringing the goods up to the workspace," Hugh Miller says as he swings open the huge weathered steel doors to reveal the second floor view down onto the street below.

Directly behind the main pulley access to this impressive Victorian Liverpool warehouse is the entrance to Hugh's workshop. Two large panelled wooden doors welcome you into a expansive room full of timber in all shapes and sizes. There are neatly stacked planks of wood, wooden floors, walls and cabinets. Tools and worktops for the construction and adaption of wood and an office space neatly constructed inside the workshop. The office flows naturally over two levels, combining a clever use of various woods, elegantly placed glass and a brilliant use of space. The current space took six full months of building and fitting out to get it to where it is now. A space he shares with his brother, an architect. He says "We wanted to use relatively cheap materials but make them look quality. It forced us to think creatively to get the most out of the wood."

Hugh knew from an early age that he wanted to build things, asking for a shed for his 15th birthday. He recalls the first piece he made: "I went out and bought some green oak. I made a writing desk. Not knowing the nature of timber, it dried and warped all over the place – I was fascinated by the material and I've been obsessed with timber ever since."

He studied architecture at university to Masters level, giving him a great overview of the process, from initial concepts through to build. "I loved the MA but it also showed me that I didn't want to become an architect." After a short time in London he started a workshop in Chester, then last year moved to the current space in Liverpool, where he takes on a variety of projects with timber, saying "I like to do one architectural job a year. My main work is commissioned furniture and the newest string is speculative pieces that I will be exhibiting next year." For his speculative pieces he likes to use home grown timber from the UK, sourcing from a number of specialised saw mills.

> *"I loved the MA but it also showed me that I didn't want to become an architect."*

Walking around the workshop there are a number of handmade pieces that immediately catch our eye. One such piece was the record bureau made from Iroko wood with a 1985 Bang and Olufusen turntable seamlessly sunken into the top. The console, like other stunning pieces, have a folded aesthetic creating a flow and natural movement. Hugh says "the grain is a sign of where the timber is strong, so my designs follow this. I love timber. There is something haptic and visceral about it. It's light enough to pick up but strong enough to hold things. It's a cruel mistress if you don't use it in the way it should be used. There really aren't two pieces the same."

This passion for timber is clear to see in all of Hugh's work. Maybe it's the architectural training that allows him to produce these unique shapes and experiment with different timber. Maybe it's his obvious love for the materials. Or just that he's an exceptionally talented wood craftsman. Whatever it is, he is producing beautiful pieces of handmade furniture that are as unique as the wood that flows through them.

PAUL SARGENT
ALFRED SARGENT SHOES

—

www.alfredsargent.co.uk

Bacon, beans and fried egg, cooked on the camping stove overlooking a lake, is the perfect way to start the day. We are in Northamptonshire, the heart of the world-renowned English shoemaking region, to meet Paul Sargent from Alfred Sargent shoes, a fourth generation shoemaker. Alfred Sargent has been synonymous with quality English shoemaking since 1899. We met Paul at the company's premises in Rushden, Northamptonshire, a spot it has occupied for over 100 years.

We follow an external green 'office' sign up a few stairs and ring the bell. Moments later the black door swings open and Paul greets us. He takes us straight into the factory and walks us through the journey of the shoe, from design patterns to the fully-assembled shoe. The first room we head into has cutting patterns of the different shoes and layers of leather hide stacked on shelving units. Through some double doors, we are in the large factory space.

Single storey, open plan and full of activity, different noises ring out from the different machines, with highly skilled craftsmen cutting, assembling, shaping and hand printing the famous Alfred Sargent shoe, step-by-step, technique after technique. Paul says, "making shoes is an art assisted by the machine. Everyone here is highly skilled at what they do." He talks us through each stage with a detail that only a lifetime of shoe making can allow, sharing with us Northampton's past, the factory's shoe making history and a process that hasn't changed that much over the years.

Alfred Sargent started the business with his two sons Frank and Harry, back in 1899. Frank, Paul's grandfather, was in charge of selling, while Harry was the technician because he had trained at Rolls Royce. The factory was geared up to export to America but, with the onset of the Second World War, all of the factories were commandeered to make army boots, so each factory had to change production and product. After the war, Paul's father took over the business and it wasn't until 1964, after studying at college, that Paul came into the family business. He learned quickly saying, "I worked in every department, so I could use all the machinery and fully understand the process." Paul now oversees all the output, ensuring high standards are always met. The team he has around him has years of experience. Paul says, "most of these people have been here a long time, some are second and third generation. They either stay here six months or go out in a box. Shoe making's in the blood in this area."

This group of master craftsmen, under the watchful eye of Paul Sargent, continues to produce and hand finish shoes using the same techniques as generations of Sargents have done for over a century. Paul says, "for me it's a passion. I believe you have to enjoy what you do, but the real satisfaction comes from a customer who puts on a shoe and is really happy with the fit and the feel." This dedication, focus and years of experience means that whatever shoe you choose from the Alfred Sargent collection, you can ensure quality craftsmanship from heel to toe.

"They either stay here six months or go out in a box. Shoe making's in the blood in this area."

———

PETER ZAIN
LEVERITT
WORKHOUSE CLOTHING

———

www.workhouse-england.co.uk

Standing at the end of a row of residential houses in Bury St Edmunds, we find the studio we are looking for: a single storey building, half painted black, with wooden steps to the entrance. Iggi swings open the door and greets us with a beaming smile, introducing his wife Ryoko. They co-own Workhouse Clothing, working from the old Victorian slaughterhouse they have restored, repaired and reclaimed, since 2011.

We enter through on old door put together with close to 50 individual pieces of wood. In front of us is a re-used horse carriage, sitting under a hand-carved wooden ladder. The centre space is dominated by a large table where Iggi works designing the different ranges. Clothes are individually hung on rails and pegs around the studio and the classic Workhouse high top bowler hat sits proud on the window sill.

Workhouse is borne out of a renewed appreciation for the hidden beauty in old things. They create clothing with a certain swagger, mixing old with new, contrasting fabrics and textures, creating a look that is "formal worn informally". The inspiration Iggi tells us "comes from the Victorian street, and in particular random photographs of street traders and musicians." Looking around the room there are collections of these images pinned to the wall and next to them, press clippings, fabric tears and sketches... the whole studio feels like a den of creativity – and a very stylish one at that. One image that jumped out and followed us round the room was a shot of Oliver Reid as Bill Sykes in Oliver Twist, staring straight at the camera wearing a long coat. Iggi looks at the shot and says, "the silhouette from top to bottom is important to me. That's why I collect old photos, I get really excited by the shape and the cut of a garment. These ideas I transfer into the Workhouse range but the trick is to not to replicate these garments – I am not re-creating a period drama."

When he was younger, Iggi went to art school for a day, but left because... as he puts it "I couldn't draw". Later that year he took a trip to the London College of Fashion and decided to apply. "I borrowed a girlfriend's shirt she'd made, and I pretended it was mine. They were really impressed and I managed to get in. You've got to take your chances," he says with a smile on his face. Four years later, after graduating, Iggy entered the world of fashion, learning his trade under lots of different designers, in studios and on market stalls, finding his feet and his style.

Workhouse has evolving over the last five years, steadily growing in England, Hong Kong and Japan. The ranges appeal to buyers who appreciate the style and the focused inspiration, which is apparent everywhere, from the workshop and the images pinned to the wall, to the ever-evolving clothes and fabrics. There is a lovely tactility about a Workhouse garment. Iggi is passionate about the fabrics he uses, where he sources them from, and how he and his close-knit team put them together to create unique pieces, that are both stylish and a garment for life.

"The silhouette from top to bottom is important to me. That's why I collect old photos, I get really excited by the shape and the cut of a garment."

———

DAVID HIEATT

HIUT DENIM

———

www.hiutdenim.co.uk

"Do one thing well." This is the first line
you see on the Hiut Denim website and the
first thing you realise when you visit the
Hiut Denim factory. It is also the line that
started the 'With Love' project.

"I want to get this town making jeans again and I want to get 400 people their jobs back."

———

We are lucky enough to meet the co-founder of Hiut Denim, David Hieatt, one sunny morning, just outside Cardigan in his factory.

When we arrive at the Open Day, shortly after 10, everything is in full swing. There is an eclectic bunch of customers, jeans enthusiasts and fans of the Hiut story, waiting eagerly to discover the inner workings of this exciting company; itching to witness the process, the ideas and the people that make this innovative company tick. It is easy to forget, sometimes, that this is a company set up by David and his wife Clare not that long ago in 2011.

We are looked after by Hiut's grand masters, a highly-trained collection of individuals with decades of experience making the finest jeans. Each grand master talks us through, section by section, from the initial cutting pattern on the computer to the finished pair of Hiut Jeans we hold in our hands. At each station we find out all the intricacies of the jeans making process, from the tweaking of patterns to the cutting, stitching, ironing, riveting and finishing.

Even though Hiut is still a young company, this particular group of grand masters has years of jeans making ability between them. They are part of what makes Hiut so

special. This town used to make jeans... lots of them. 400 people used to make 35,000 pairs of jeans a week. That was until one day in 2002, when the factory had to close. This tragedy forced hundreds of experts out of work. Decades of ability was lost instantly. David is now looking to these former jeans makers to harness their skills, producing quality this time round, not quantity. Hiut allows the grand masters to individually craft each pair of jeans and then sign each one before they go out to the lucky customer.

David wants to get the town of Cardigan making jeans again and he currently employs a number of the staff from the old factory, saying "12 employed, only 388 to go." He is an ideas man, a real inspiration. He built clothing company Howies with the aim of having an ethically correct clothing company. He set up the Do Lectures, first in Wales, then in San Francisco and soon in Australia, to bring people together to share ideas, debate, listen and inspire. He turned his hand to print and digital with the Do Book Co; publishing inspirational pocket guides. His focus now is Hiut Denim, born to get the town making jeans again and to be the most creative jeans company in the world.

David says "in order to realise great ideas, you have to execute them well and then tell everyone. No-one will know how great your idea is unless you shout from the rooftops." He does this brilliantly, constantly finding unique ways to talk to the customer, sharing his ideas and his precious time with anybody who is interested.

Just like each pair of jeans they make, the Hiut Denim company is well crafted - combining creative thinking with years of experience. Through sharing stories, Hiut is building a bright future, and with the demand for its jeans increasing all the time, David's vision of getting 400 Cardigan residents making jeans again, no longer seems that farfetched.

DAVID HUNTER
THE COPPICE PLOT

———

www.thecoppiceplot.com

We had planned on camping in
David's woodland overnight, but
he calls us en route to let us know
torrential rain is forecast. The offer of
a home cooked meal and a roof over
our heads seems too good to miss...

"One day David can be felling trees in a dense section, the next he could be firing charcoal in the drum or carving wooden spoons to sell at the local markets."

———

We arrive a little later than planned; the smell of freshly baked bread and hotpot greet us. We sit around the table and eat, drink and find out all about David and the Coppice Plot.

David studied marine and environmental science at university and went on to do a Masters in conservation. After a short stint in Africa doing marine conservation he came back to London, working on a city farm. It wasn't long before he moved on again and decided, with his wife Sarah, to move out to Wales to do environmental education. While he was in Pembrokeshire, David completed a woodland management course on coppicing and learned how to make items out of wood using hand tools such as knives and axes. It was the axe work in the woods that he particularly loved and after the course decided he wanted to keep on doing it so set about finding a woods to look after and thats how he ended up at Kitewood near Fishguard, Pembrokshire.

In the morning we are up early and head over to the woodland that David manages. Coppicing is a form of forestry management, a traditional way of looking after an area of woodland and managing it to get the most out of the land. David fells sections of the forest on a rotational basis, so that when he gets back to where he started, the trees are fully grown again and the new cycle begins. Every time the trees are cut down they produce a number of products, ranging from top quality Pembrokeshire charcoal to a variety of beautiful greenwood work items, using everything and making sure nothing goes to waste. He uses two basic tools, his axe, a 1963 British-made Elwell for felling and his sickle-shaped billhook for taking off the smaller branches. These two simple tools have helped transform the forest into the sustainable area it is today.

As well as the charcoal and woodcrafts, David has helped set up Kitewood Camping on an old golf course, which was replanted 15 years ago. Now a thick woodland, the 11 plots are generously spaced in clearings within the forest; small tracks sided with long grasses and wild flowers connect the plots alongside small ponds that David has created to make sure that there is an abundance of wildlife. Each plot consists of a cleared area to pitch tents, a firepit and picnic table within the trees, complete with a tarpaulin cover to protect you from the inevitable rain. During the summer season David, his wife Sarah, son Flynn and dog Penny live onsite in a retro '70s caravan in a clearing, with a newly-planted willow fence and wood working tools in the garden. There are not many truly wild camping sites in the UK and Kitewood has to be among the finest. It really is a magical place.

David's office is the forest. He is confined only by the forest boundaries. One day he can be felling trees in a dense section, the next he could be firing charcoal in the drum or carving wooden spoons to sell at the local markets. It's a very rewarding way to earn a living, looking after a beautiful forest and maintaining its upkeep, while taking enough to earn a living and live a great life.

MELISSA COLE
ARTIST BLACKSMITH

———

www.melissacole.co.uk

Smoke from the metal chimney
spirals upwards as we approach
Melissa Cole's forge in the beautiful
Wiltshire countryside. Passing
through the white wooden doors,
we can see the flames rise as Melissa
works some steel on the anvil.

Her space – a former pig shed – is in a long, brick building. The majority of tools are set around the forge, the heart of any blacksmith's dwelling. As work spaces go, this has to be as traditional as they come, with the aged anvil sitting on a weathered tree stump. Both the anvil and the stump are covered in layers of ingrained soot through years of use. Just like the anvil and stump, the majority of tools are also made with wood and metal and hang within reach of the forge, ready to be used at any moment. Melissa points out some wrought iron she has salvaged from a local church saying, "that would have been forged in the 17th century using the same techniques as I do now and I can use that metal to create something new. Repeating this old process is a lovely experience."

Melissa was introduced to blacksmithing by her dad, who taught metal work and ran his own forge. He was a traditional blacksmith but let her experiment, from the tender age of seven, under his watchful eye. She says, "I remember making snakes and tent pegs, just learning the basics. It wasn't until my late teens that I experimented a bit more and knew I wanted to pursue a creative career, but I wasn't exactly sure in what." After working with ceramics and plastics at university she found her way to metal, where she felt more at home. "I've always been very comfortable with metal. It is just such an expressive medium. I felt that this was more 'me'."

Her dad took early retirement and built a bigger workshop for himself with two forges, which gave Melissa the opportunity to continue her work with metal. She took it. She made a chair for her sister as a wedding present, then was asked to make another for someone else, then curtain poles and various other items for people who appreciated her artistic style. Working with her dad allowed Melissa to polish her traditional blacksmith skills, but also allowed her free time to be creative. She wanted to spread the idea of being creative with metal and developed a community art scheme for local schools. This involved taking her mobile forge into schools to teach blacksmithing skills. It was a huge success. "I have worked with thousands of children and visited over 35 school and community groups across the south of England."

In 2007 Melissa was awarded a prestigious 'Bronze Medal' from The Worshipful Company of Blacksmiths (an authority set up in 1325 to support blacksmiths that use traditional techniques), in recognition of the blacksmithing skills seen in her public and private work and the successful 'Forging-in-schools' project. Melissa still runs workshops and courses but fits them in around commissions and sculpture work. Indeed, she set up a gallery in a nearby converted barn to show her work, as well as those of other selected artists. She talks us through a beautiful selection of her steel, iron and bronze work that combine traditional forging techniques with elegant, flowing fine art designs. It was great to see the final pieces and every stage of the process is fascinating. We flick through her notebook, bursting with sketches of ideas, flowing lines and notes – the starting point for all her pieces. We then see Melissa working with steel heated to a yellow glow in the forge, skilfully manipulating it into shape with hammer and anvil. It became two linked hearts... a present for us to take away.

We had already met a traditional blacksmith, producing metal work for practical solutions, so it is great to see those same forging techniques and hammer work used to produce something completely different – metal work that flows and wraps around itself, taking your eyes on a journey; pieces that are solid in make up but light and free in their aesthetic quality. It is possible to see every physical mark made by Melissa with every blow of the hammer, recreating her original 2D sketches with hot metal, hammer and anvil to produce a truly unique piece of art.

WE ARE DEDI

CATED

—

TO FINDING PEOPLE WHO
PRODUCE THINGS WITH A
PASSION AND A PURPOSE.

NORMAN YAP
NORMAN YAP CERAMICS

—

www.normanyapceramics.com

On his 40th birthday Norman Yap received a book that changed the direction of his life forever, moving him away from the major corporations and into the world of ceramics. The book, Susan Peterson's 'Art and Craft of Clay,' inspired him to become a professional potter and his drive and ambition allowed that dream to become a reality.

Norman worked in major corporations as a management consultant for many years, but a merger and acquisition at his last workplace gave him the opportunity to step away from that career altogether. He had always appreciated art, especially ceramics, and, encouraged by his partner, he enrolled in pottery classes. It was clear from an early stage that he had made the right choice but Norman knew he couldn't get everything he needed from the classes alone. He moved quickly into a studio share, surrounding himself with skilled potters and learning through observation and absorption.

He meets us at the door of his workshop with a big smile on his face. His clothes are flecked with clay and he gives us the grand tour. His studio is long and thin with high ceilings. Vases and pots are lined up on shelves, different glazes stacked next to each other and a number of potters wheels poised, ready to be put to work. We catch Norman in the middle of a production run, so we wipe down some chairs and sit down to find out more about his work.

He recalls the first time he created a piece with his unique style. "I was two years in and had made a porcelain bowl that I'd altered by squeezing the top. My partner took one look and said, 'That's it! That's your style! You're never selling this piece.'" It's still in the house to this day. The 'altered' top is one of many subtle details that are evident throughout Norman's work. These details have caught the eye of many collectors and helped his work appear for sale in galleries such as Tate Britain and National Galleries of Scotland.

He specialises in thrown stoneware and porcelain and we are lucky enough to see some pieces in his showroom. The blue/green glaze on his stoneware pieces catch my eye first and the copper red bursts on the porcelain work beautifully. These colour combinations have been used for over 3,000 years and are perfected using a reduction gas fired kiln which is rare in London, mainly due to ventilation regulations. This technique is very hands-on, but allows Norman to produce the various finishes that other techniques wouldn't allow. He says "The feel of a piece is very important to me – some forms have a gritty texture to go with the mottled glazes but I like to keep porcelain forms clean, smooth and minimally glazed."

Outside his studio, he is passionate about the craft world creating opportunities for people to sell, exhibit and make themselves known, bringing attention to the craft industry. He sits on the London Potters Council and is part of the Society for Designer Craftsmen. He says "In the current climate it's very hard for a maker to survive. It's also very hard for colleges who teach these skills to survive. If we don't take care of what we know and act as custodians for the knowledge that is being passed down, then these skills die very easily."

Norman is softly spoken but passionate and confident in his delivery. We sit together, relaxed, surrounded by work in different stages of completion, as he says: "The onus of the maker is to make things to the best of their ability, making sure the craft remains alive and very up to date. What started me off at the beginning is what still keeps me going. I get ideas in my head, I get forms and they kind of taunt me saying; 'Come on – make me! Make me!'" It's these forms – the clean lines; the fabulous colours; the unique pieces – that keep people interested; keep people collecting and keep people exhibiting his work. This in turn gives Norman the freedom to keep producing unique pieces for everyone to experience and enjoy.

"I was two years in and I had made a porcelain bowl that I altered by squeezing the top. My partner took one look and said, "That's it! That's your style, your never selling this piece."

———

MATTHEW SOWTER
SAFFRON FRAMEWORKS

———

www.saffronframeworks.com

Preparing modern cuisine for fine diners
and creating bespoke cycles in a London
workshop may seem worlds apart. But,
back in 2009, Matthew Sowter swapped
his chef's whites for an oily overall to start
making bicycles at Enigma, before setting
up Saffron Frameworks.

"Customers love the opportunity to come to the workshop, to smell the metal and oil and touch and feel the different materials. It's a very tactile process."

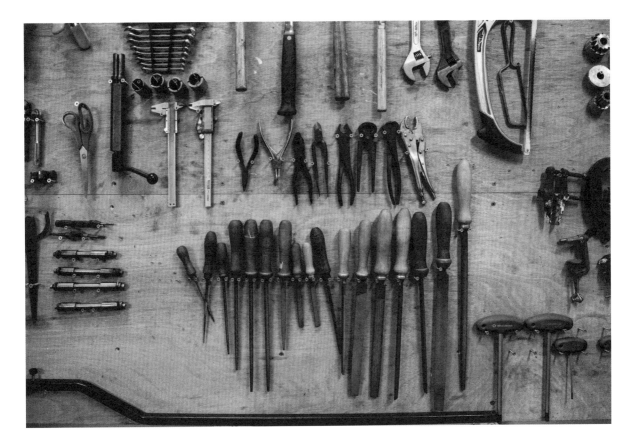

Matthew has always loved bikes, racing them on and off-road from an early age. But, back in 2009, an illness stopped him riding, stopped him working and even stopped him getting out of bed for over a month. Faced with time to decide what he wanted from life, he stumbled across an article about an Italian frame builder called Darren Chrisp. Matthew says: "Reading about Darren's ethos on why he made frames and the process he goes through really inspired me. That was the catalyst." He picked up the phone and spoke to Darren, finding out all he could about the bike-making process. He knew then was hooked and he that making bikes was his future.

He quickly got a job with Enigma Bikes, learning his trade, sharpening his skills and soaking up all he could about the frame building process. This invaluable experience opened his world up and just over two years ago he set up Saffron Frameworks, a place where he creates bespoke, functional and beautiful looking bikes, for customers all over the world.

His work allows him to create real connections with his clients. He believes in a collaborative process, saying "customers love the opportunity to come to the workshop, to smell the metal and oil and touch and feel the different materials, it's a very tactile process." It is this process that ensures each bike is built to the exact needs of the cyclist. "I source my tubes from all over the world – there are literally thousands I can choose from, mix and matching tubing to give the person the best quality for their ride. Everything is tailored, from the frame right down to the smallest screw."

It is this attention to detail that has seen customers buy bikes from all over the world, from as far away as Singapore. It has also helped him to pick up Best Bicycle awards from the likes of Spin London and Bespoked Bristol. His bikes are highly sought-after and there is currently a six month waiting list, which – for someone who has only been building bikes for five years – is a great feat. Each commission brings another exciting collaboration and unique output that keeps Matthew motivated, constantly pushing the boundaries, learning new techniques and honing skills in a trade that he loves and truly believes in.

SIMON DAY
NOCTURNE WORKSHOP

———

www.nocturneworkshop.com

The light burst out from the workshop,
illuminating the dark courtyard
in front of us. The shutter was up;
Nocturne Workshop's Simon Day was
busy working on a lamp shade, before
glancing up and welcoming us in.

Modernist, bespoke handmade lighting is Nocturne's speciality, alongside equally individual handmade furniture. Several Deco-inspired pieces give a nod to the past, but Simon's work clearly has one eye on the future too looking at one of his latest pieces. A dynamic, angular metal light is suspended form the ceiling, lit with LED strips. "I've always loved the way lights can transform spaces," he says. And the lamps in his workshop do that beautifully. One at a time though – Simon only has one lightbulb in the whole workshop.

It was in college that Simon was introduced to welding using a 1950s oil-filled Oxford Welder. "It was pretty brutal welding, but gave me a new love for working with steel," he says. This steel and metal work can be seen throughout Simon's work. There is an honesty in his design – pieces that are made well and made to last: stripped-back design with industrial detailing. "I always make sure the design is informed by its function" he says.

From college, he started work restoring lighting and furniture, learning a lot through Victorian workshop manuals, understanding the techniques and equipment used when these pieces were originally produced. He says

"This gave me the chance to take things apart and put them back together again, giving me a great understanding of how things worked. It also allowed me to have physical relationship with pieces that would usually just sit in people's homes or placed in museums."

Simon started producing lamps after work and in 2011 Nocturne was born. He knows to establish himself as a world-renowned lighting designer will take years, but is happy producing bespoke creations, perfecting his craft and constantly taking influence from the world around him, illuminating spaces and transforming rooms with his own unique eye for detail and creative flair.

GREG ROWLAND
ROWLAND WHEELWRIGHTS

———

www.wheelwrightsshop.com

It was a beautiful day as we pulled up
the drive to Rowland Wheelwrights.
Through the windscreen of the Landy
we can see three people moving a loom.
Greg is the first to notice us and heads
out to say hello. He passes below the
Royal Coat of Arms hanging high above
the entrance and introduces us to his dad
Mike and George, his young apprentice.

Greg has taken over this 700 year old family business from his father Mike. The business can be traced back to the building of Exeter Cathedral in 1331, when Rowland Wheelwright's carts carried stone from Beer Quarry to the building site. He takes us round the workshop past traditional carts, stacked wooden wheels and a selection of cannons, which certainly catch our attention. He tells us that his dad started here in 1964. Mike originally trained as a joiner but, to make extra money, he'd go out and "fix wagons with the gypsies." His father is a yeoman wheelwright and Greg is a master wheelwright... a title which was bestowed on him by the Lord Mayor of London, no less. He says "I've been trained by my father and he still gives me little nuggets of wisdom." As we talk to Greg, his father is busy working round the corner. Even at 78, he shows no sign of slowing down, spending five or six days a week in the workshop.

Greg has a unique skill set. He joined the trade after five years in the army, where he qualified as a Land Rover mechanic. He is also a trained blacksmith, as well as a wheelwright, and he fits in being a local fireman when needed. He's worked 25 years in the wheelwright trade and is very excited to have one of only two wheelwrights apprentices in the country. He can now pass down the skills he's learnt from his dad to a new generation. Today, George the apprentice is working with Mike round the corner and is relishing the challenge of his three year apprenticeship, where he will learn a wide range of skills. In the short time we are there, Greg shows us a huge number of wheels, all different sizes and thicknesses; some plain wood and metal, some ornately painted. There are cannons, wagons and even a wooden bike.

The sheer variety of work that George has to master requires a huge amount of different tools. There are shelves stacked high with boxes full to bursting; tools we recognised and tools that are handmade for specific purposes, some looking like they were used every day and others covered in cobwebs. Greg points to one high up on a shelf and says "I've not used that for years, but I know I'll need it for a job in the future. George will have to use most of these tools and probably have to make some of his own."

The workshop is always busy, most years producing between 150 and 200 hand-crafted, finished and painted wheels. Occasionally though, they get an order that has to jump to the top of the list, because it has been made 'By Royal Request'. Rowland Wheelwright's is one of only two companies that look after carriages for the Queen, which clearly demonstrates the level of workmanship that goes on here. They also currently specialise in military equipment but Greg says, "the market is always changing and we adapt to the demand for our work."

The variety of work is clear to see all around the workshop and it is obvious Greg loves it all, saying, "I do it because it's in my blood, I can't imagine not doing it."

From wheels to carriages, wooden bikes to cannons, it is great to witness the process involved, the techniques needed and the materials used to keep this very traditional trade alive. It's even better to see those skills being passed on to a new generation of wheel-building talent.

DAVE SMITH
ORNAMENTAL GLASS ARTIST

———

www.davidadriansmith.com

Based in his home studio in Torquay, Dave Smith blurs
the lines between art and trade. His distinctive designs
can be seen all over the world, from album covers for the
Kings of Leon to bottle art for Jameson Whiskey. His
more traditional sign work can be seen all over the UK,
particularly adorning many London pubs and bars.

Dave welcomes us in to the studio next to his house and walking in you can't help but smile. A mass of stunning mirrored sign pieces, hand-etched framed artwork and glass engravings line the walls. The light bounces around the room off the gold leaf, mirrors and glass signs, illuminating different visual delights everywhere you look. A quick glance around reveals hand-drawn signs for Burberry and for Booths; mirrored signs from pubs and hand-drawn pieces, attached to the exposed wooden beams. It truly is a creative's dream.

The detail of Dave's work is stunning and we are keen to find out how long it takes to get this good. Dave recalls the first sign he made, "I was 14 at the time and I painted a sign for my dad's friend, a hotel owner in Torquay. I used all the wrong tools and the wrong paints, but the sign still looked pretty good. I was hooked from there on in." That sign led to other signs and, by the time he was 16, his dad had managed to get him on an apprenticeship scheme in a traditional sign maker's. He says "It was run by an ex-sergeant major, who ran a tight ship and I questioned whether I would stick it out, but I was so passionate and surrounded by professionals I just wanted to learn more."

Whilst at the company Dave produced hand-drawn signs for shops, pubs and, one year, the All England Tennis Club at Wimbledon. The apprenticeship lasted five to six years, just before the digital age, when vinyl sign writing started to take over from traditional hand lettering. "I used to sign write and paint logos straight onto the side of vans. They were great days – everything hand-brushed with writing quills or, sometimes, screen printed."

As well as the four day apprenticeship, Dave had to spend a day in college. But the local college didn't have a sign writing course – the closest thing was a dress making course. So, as well as designing beautiful hand-drawn signs, Dave can also mend your corset, or fix a special dress. He chuckles as he recalls the course and then told us about the next few years. "I wanted to learn all of the techniques, travelling extensively to learn different processes. I spent some time in America on courses and events learning everything I could. I wanted to learn the process for guilding, cutting, silvering, and sign writing acid etching and bring it all together as one." Dave tells us one person made a real difference to his world back then, a man called Rick Glawson. "He opened doors to some amazing opportunities in glass and design for me, which allowed me to meet some wonderfully talented people who crossed my path and later become friends."

> *"I love what I do, I just wouldn't do anything else. It's nice now to just get out of bed, wander down and start creating..."*

———

Rather surprisingly for a hand-drawn signwriter Dave says "the rise of the digital age definitely helped the business. I'd still always start with the pencil, making sure 60-70% of the work is done by hand, but then the rest by the computer." He set up and ran his own business for 15 years, before deciding to sell up and work from the space he occupies now at the side of his house. He says "I love what I do, I just wouldn't do anything else. It's nice now to just get out of bed, wander down and start creating."

Dave's wide skill set means his work is so varied. He goes to a bookshelf and pulls out a vinyl cover he produced for John Mayer – it's a blend of beautiful typography and flowing design,

creating a stunning hand-rendered piece of art. Then he grabs a whiskey bottle that he created for a limited run of Jameson and unrolls a design he is just finishing for Disney. The list of work produced for notable names is a very long one, but this acclaim hasn't affected his warm, welcoming personality. Dave is an incredibly talented and humble person. It is an absolute pleasure to share an afternoon with him, listen to stories and get a small glimpse into his world.

PAUL MEARS
MEARS BOAT BUILDERS

www.mearsboatbuilders.co.uk

Mears Boat Builders was one of our first finds at the With Love Project and we've looked forward to meeting the family behind the beautiful wooden boats for a good while. This year, the business is celebrating 71 years of success and has moved on to the third generation, as Alex Mears takes over from his father Paul.

We arrive to find Paul up a ladder mending a 20ft boat outside his workshop. Paul is in his 70s now and has been making boats here for years. He jumps down from the ladder and leads us into the workshop, which sits on the edge of an estuary and is less than 200 metres from the ocean. It's a great space with a high roof and pulley systems hanging from metal beams. There's a half-built wooden boat sitting at the back and hundreds of tools hung and placed in specific order. He shows us around and tells us the business moved here in 1982, just a stone's throw from their old shed, which his father had occupied from 1957. Before that, Paul's dad had a place over in Beer, converted from an old grain store, that he started working from in 1945.

For as long as he can remember, Paul has always loved wood, spending time every day in his dad's workshop. He says... "we had to walk past my dad's workshop on the way back from school and a friend and I would always go in and nick a few bits of wood, throw them in the brook nearby and race them all the way down to the beach." He started working with his dad when

he was 15, but it wasn't until he was 18 that he built his first wooden boat. His dad learned his trade in Exmouth working for Ron Lavis in the years before the war, then for Dixons during the first couple of years of the war until he became foreman building wooden MFVs (Military Fishing Vessel) in Topsham during the remainder of the war. He had a great working relationship with him, saying "my dad was brilliant to work under, he could turn his hand to most things – metal work, plumbing, electrical work – but he was a real master when it came to using wood. I was constantly learning from him. I'm still learning now, every day."

At their height they were building three or four wooden boats a year with around five people working for them, one of whom pops in just as the kettle boils. Graham still lives in the town and worked with Paul at the boat yard years ago. He's in his 70s now and loves a good brew and chat at the workshop. With nearly 100 years of experience combined, Paul and Graham have some great stories to tell about the boat making business. We perch ourselves on one of the wooden work

benches with a brew and it is an absolute pleasure to listen to the two of them. Graham is just one of a steady flux of people popping in and out during our visit to the workshop or, as Paul calls it, "the town's community centre".

Paul has three sons, two of whom, he says, are "smart as anything, but give them a hammer and a nail and they haven't a clue what to do with them. The third one though, Alex, is bloody good with wood." Alex joined the firm following a five year honours degree in structural engineering. He is away at the time of our visit, picking a boat up from Scotland. Paul says "He may be taking over but he'll have to get used to me being around. Retirement just isn't for me, I've tried golf but the bats are far too bloody small."

Paul used to be down at the shed until 9pm at night most days, but now, he tells us, his back lets him know it's time to go home about 3:30. It is clear this isn't just a job for Paul, but a way of life. Surrounded by boats and friends popping in for a brew, the smell of fresh sea air wafts in through the open doors; personal projects sit close at hand, with years of tinkering left in them. Even with Alex taking over the business, it's obvious Paul won't be putting his feet up any time soon.

"*Stick to what you enjoy
and you'll end up doing
something you love.*"

—

James Otter - Otter Surfboards

JAMES OTTER
OTTER SURFBOARDS

———

www.ottersurfboards.co.uk

We camp right next to Otter Surfboards
in the Mount Pleasant Eco Park and,
after a freshly-brewed coffee and bacon
butty made on the single burner, we
head over to meet James Otter.

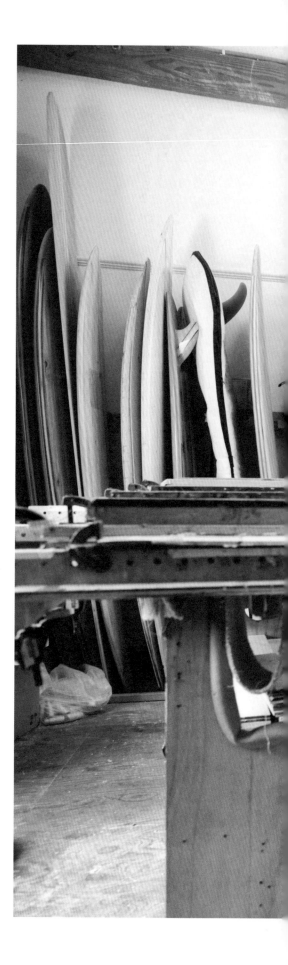

The door to the double height workshop is open, but Buddy, the black Lab, blocks our path. He barks to say hello and alerts the guys busy working that we've arrived.

Otter Surfboards have been producing beautiful hollow, skin and frame wooden surfboards from their workshop in Cornwall since 2010. Barefoot, James greets us and invites us in. The methodical sound of hand saws echo around the workshop and the occasional whirr of the band sander ramps up as the team prepare for the following day's open day and upcoming workshops. The space houses a number of gnarled worktop benches, perfectly hung tools and plenty of wooden surfboards. Some are racked up, leaning against each other while some are presented like works of art, resting proudly on wooden pegs fixed to the wall. There is a chalk board with the upcoming local wave information on and Buddy the Lab is ever-present.

James grew up near London, but would always holiday near the coast and got hooked on surfing from an early age. That love of the coast heavily influenced his decision for university, studying design and making at Plymouth. It was in his final year in Plymouth that his first wooden surfboard was produced. James carried on making the surfboards after university in his spare time, whilst working as a carpenter. Fifteen boards and a number of years later, James had a process he was happy with and decided to go full time, producing great boards that are as ethically and environmentally sound as possible. Asked why he concentrates on producing boards as opposed to other forms of carpentry he says, "I guess it harks back to what my father said to me... stick to what you enjoy and you'll end up doing something you love."

This very process is now available for anyone who wants to learn how to make a wooden board. James and the team deliver workshops which invite people to make surfboards with them and learn all the techniques as they produce their very own handmade surfboard. James says, "I love the workshops, they bring a new excitement and energy every time." In the world of business, where people rarely truly share a process, this whole experience is certainly refreshing and the results are stunning boards, happy customers and shared great experiences.

As well as looking like pieces of art, the wood offers a natural connection to the environment that foam boards can't. Whether it's a workshop built board or hand made by James himself you can guarantee each has its own personality and uniqueness, brought about by the locally-sourced materials, hand-crafted process and the passion put into construction.

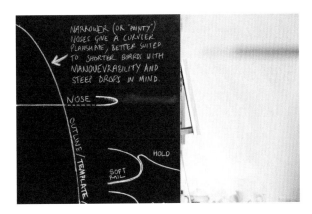

TOM KAY
FINISTERRE

———

www.finisterre.com

We sit on the ragged ox blood Chesterfield, with surf images hanging above our heads. Tom from Finisterre descends the wooden stairs in the workshop and puts the kettle on, gesturing for us to join him; we jump up and park ourselves in the open plan kitchen.

Finisterre is a clothing brand based in Cornwall, born from the needs of hardy British surfers, pushing innovation and product development in the surf industry. In their words, they produce "functional and sustainable products with a strong sense of style for those who share a love of the sea." That love of the sea is something Tom remembers from an early age; he spent many of his early years on the north coast of Norfolk but didn't get into surfing until he was nearly 17. Once he did, he was hooked and this became his passion. He continued surfing at university where he was studying marine biology, but realised he didn't want to become a scientist.

It was his passion for surfing on these shores and his love for the coast that led him to set up Finisterre. "I was flicking through a surf mag when I saw a black and white photograph of a surfer taking off on a huge, cold 30ft wave – it stopped me in my tracks. The preparation both physically and mentally to get to that very point takes serious commitment and I knew I wanted to create a brand that represented this kind of commitment. Since day one we've committed to product, people and the environment."

With blind naivety, optimistic drive and serious conviction, Tom set about making Finisterre happen. He says "In the beginning you don't have the perfect business model or the financial fire power to compete, but what you do have is determination and belief." He set about building a brand that would make innovative, sustainable products and in 2008 the company won the Observer ethical business award with a range that included recycled polyester jackets, organic cotton and Merino wool base layers. Shortly after, they started looking at ways to bring their manufacturing back to the UK. Some of their product line is made from their unique blend of Merino wool, some which comes from Australia and New Zealand. The idea was to create a UK supply chain, grown, spun, woven and manufactured into product right here. This focus led them to Lesley Prior in Devon, with her flock of Bowmont sheep.

The story of the Bowmont sheep goes back to the 1970s. The Macaulay Breeding Institute wanted to create a UK breed to rival the fine wool from the Merino sheep of New Zealand and Australia, that would survive in the UK. In order to achieve it they crossed a Saxon Merino, known for its super fine fibre, with a hardy Shetland breed, fully acclimatised to the harsh UK weather. The result was an acclimatised sheep with a fine fibre, necessary for soft handle garments. Unfortunately funding soon ran out and the programme was abandoned. For the Bowmont breed, this led to a rapid

decline. Fast forward 20 years and Lesley Prior took it on herself to collect the only remaining pure bred Bowmonts in the land – 29 sheep in total. The last seven or eight years has seen Lesley and Finisterre work together to boost Bowmont flock numbers to more than 260. Finisterre now produces a limited edition range of Bowmont sweaters, made through a 100% UK supply chain.

The passionate crew in the workshop – a stone's throw from the crashing surf in St. Agnes – live and breathe the brand. Their devotion is such that the whole team will go off to remote coasts to find waves, living in an old Swedish army tent with a wood burner. They search for unbelievable, uncrowded waves and, with the wind howling and the sea freezing, they come up with product ideas. They cook their own food, live for the surfing, test the product and spend time together as a Finisterre family. It's this commitment and focus that attracted us to Finisterre and it's what sets them apart from lots of other lifestyle brands. Buying Finisterre products means knowing you're investing in items that have been created, tested and ethically produced with a real passion and a focus on delivering the best that they can possibly be; products that will stand the test of time.

"In the beginning you don't have the perfect business model or the financial fire power to compete, but what you do have is determination and belief"

FRED JOURDEN
BLITZ MOTORCYCLES

——

www.blitz-motorcycles.com

A quick leap across the English Channel
takes us to Paris, where we jump at the
chance to meet Fred from Blitz.
For someone who didn't pass their
motorcycle test until they were 30, Fred
Jourden – one half of Blitz motorcycles
– is fast making a name for himself in the
custom-built motorcycle market.

We see Fred one drizzly day in Paris. The dullness of the day can't dampen our excitement about meeting the people behind the brilliant Blitz Motorcycles. Fred meets us outside a Paris dealership; there is no 'Blitz' sign in sight. He takes us through a noisy garage – somewhere, hidden in the back, is the Blitz workshop. We enter through a waiting area full of bike paraphernalia; tanks hang from the ceiling, engine parts are strewn around, there are vintage posters on the walls and a couple of Barcelona chairs to sit on.

Next to this waiting area is the workshop, the room were the Blitz energy and creativity lives. It has everything you would expect and more – a series of bikes at every stage of assembly; masses of tools; bike parts; shelves stacked high and grease everywhere. You get the feeling that this space has evolved around Fred and Hugo over the years – a space that works with them and allows their creativity to flow.

Fred Jourden bought his first bike, a vintage BMW, at 28. His friends told him it would break down, so he decided to enrol on a mechanics course, so that he could fix things himself should anything ever happen. However, the BMW has never broken down. "I still have it and I still ride it," he says, with a smile on his face. The course was a degree

"We take out all the fat and just leave the muscle. For us, a motorcycle is just an engine with two wheels, a tank for gasoline and a seat for your arse. That's it."

———

course, taking place after work. As soon as the clock turned 5:45 he would jump on the BMW and head over to school to sit down and get working with his hands. He says: "For me, the idea was to gain new skills, but as soon as I brought my first machine to life – a 40 year old Royal Enfield – I experienced a thrill from the top of my spine to the bottom of my feet. That moment I felt like God, 'I have given life to something.' My life changed right there and then."

Although Fred was a latecomer to the motorcycle world, Hugo Jezegabel, the other half of Blitz, has worked on bikes from childhood. They met by chance, started to share a workshop and custom built bikes for friends, learning from each other, one bike at a time. It wasn't long before they were spending more and more time at the workshop and,

eventually, decided to leave their jobs and concentrate on forming a business together. They started Blitz in the spring of 2010, choosing the name from a US Football strategy called 'the blitz', when additional players are sent to 'rush the quarterback' – a concentration of force at high speed to tackle or disrupt.

Currently they have 15 customers a year and can work on up to five machines at any one time, making sure they spend quality time with each customer to fully understand their requirements. It can be a long process, but it definitely works. "To begin with, the customer comes to us with a machine, or we find one for them," Fred says. They then strip it apart, completely dismantling the bike; no screw or bolt left holding anything together. Then they start on the creation, changing the frame, adapting the tank and creating another Blitz bespoke motorcycle. "We design by eye, no sketches, no computer. If a part doesn't look right we take it off. We keep doing that until we are happy. If we think a Kawasaki tank looks good on a Yamaha bike then we go for it."

The bikes they produce are stripped back. There is nothing on them that doesn't need to be there. Fred says, "we take out all the fat and just leave the muscle. For us, a motorcycle is just an engine with two wheels, a tank for gasoline and a seat for your arse. That's it." The combination of an original tank, sitting on the framework of matte black paint, with an exposed engine gives each machine its raw, unique Blitz look. This keeps the steady flow of interested customers knocking at their door and increases interest in their brand. "We do what we do for us and for the customer who trusts us." So far over 50 people have trusted Hugo and Fred to create a bespoke motorcycle just for them and all of them are happy with the results. It is easy to see why. The time, the creativity, the skills and the focus involved in each project mean that each bike is as unique as the customer they are produced for.

When we first arrive, Fred says: "I freeze my ass off in winter, I roast in summer, I cut my hands to shreds, wreck my clothes, but I love what I do, passion is the only reason I am here. Hugo is exactly the same."

It is this passion that drives them to do what they do, creating beautiful unique bikes again and again. Fifty satisfied customers would certainly agree.

MAKING

THIS BOOK POSSIBLE...

GF SMITH
PAPER MERCHANTS

———

www.gfsmith.com

The nature of this project has passion and purpose at its heart, so we needed to find a paper merchant who shared the same ethos. One name jumped out instantly, GF Smith, the UK's leading supplier of exclusive and creative papers to the design and print communities. So, we contacted the paper queen of the north, Jane Crowther, and set up a meeting.

Jane whisks us over to Hull, to meet the team and talk paper. They have been based there since 1885 when George Frederick Smith set up the company. By all accounts he travelled with an almost obsessive energy, by land and sea, to seek out the very finest paper manufacturers of his day. A focus that continues to this day and is delivered through a shared vision across a company pushing its love of paper and its possibilities.

Jane takes us on a tour of the headquarters; we meet people foil blocking, hand making envelopes, collating and printing books, we spend time in the paper warehouse and hitch a ride on the fork lift truck 30ft up in the air. Everyone we meet is passionate about what they do and happy to chat us through their work. Jane says "we have a great team. More than 30 people working here have been with the company 20 years or more."

The fit is perfect – a privately-owned company with a fantastic history, loyal passionate staff and a reputation for creativity and innovation. From the start of the project we knew we wanted GF Smith involved and are so thankful to them for coming on board and to Jane for having faith in us.

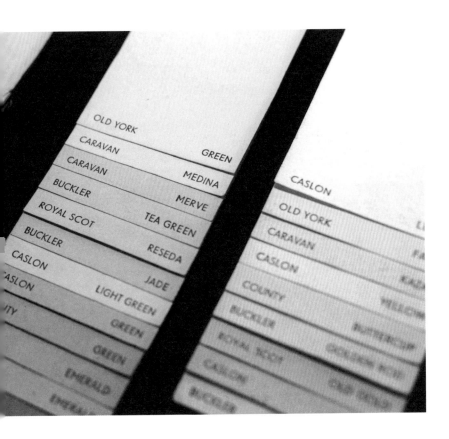

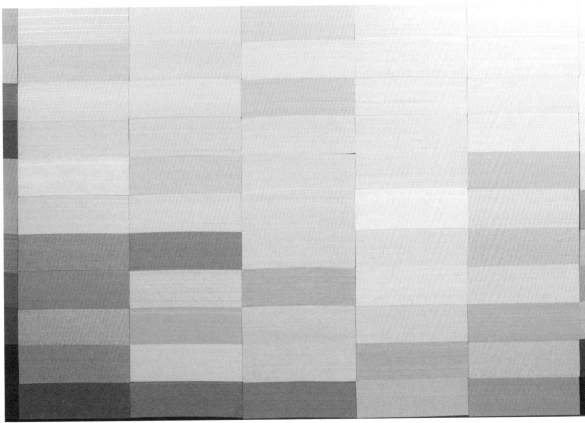

TEAM IMPRESSION
PRINTERS

———

www.team-impression.com

With our paper merchant firmly in place, we head to Leeds to meet up with Simon Bucktrout, sales director at Team Impression printers. They have a great reputation and have grown to become one of the most trusted names in print in the UK.

We arrive at Team and head to the reception area to wait for Simon. I grab a few books from the selection stacked on the shelf – one of them is photographer Rankin's book, from his 'Alive: In The Face of Death' exhibition. It is beautifully printed; a hard bound book full of stunning photography and punchy colours. We knew then – if it was good enough for Rankin, then...

Simon greets us and gives us the grand tour. He started Team back in 2001, with a small number of other print professionals who all shared a love for great print and customer service. The company has grown steadily over the years and now employs almost 100 people, providing in-house solutions in every area of print, from litho to digital, display, presentation and packaging – all under one roof.

We witness a number of the processes, from foil blocking to digital solutions; binding to cutting. But, most importantly, we meet the skilled litho staff who will be making sure our book is printed perfectly. They talk and walk us through the job from start to finish, showing us the checks, the proofing and all the stages the book will go through before it lands in our laps.

It is easy to see why Team is a favourite with the creative industries and why end users such as Reiss, Urban Splash, Tate Modern and Rankin trust them with print. Most importantly for us, we see how interested they are in getting involved with our project. We are so grateful to Simon and the team for getting involved. For the print lovers out there, Team Impression have screen printed the outer sleeve, foil blocked the cover (which is cloth over board), thread sewn the inner pages and Litho printed the book on a B1 press. We hope you enjoy the results...

THE INDIVIDUALS
KICKSTARTER PLEDGERS

———

*Thank you to everyone who made this possible. We
hope you enjoy the book...*

ACHIM
ADAM BODINI
ADAM CANAY
ADAM SLATER
ADAM STOREY
AJ
AJOTO
ALASTAIR MATTHEWS
ALEX HOGGARTH
ALEX MEARS
ALEX RIZOS
ALI DOVER
ANDREA HOLDEN
ANDREW CONNOLLY
ANDREW ECCLES
ANDREW GOLPYS
ANDREW HALDANE
ANDREW MALLALIEU
ANDY BROWN
ANDY ELLISON
ANDY FOSTER
ANITA LOVELAND
ANNA BROWN
ANNEMARIE VAN OMMEN
ANTHONY OWEN
ARRAN CROSS
BANTON FRAMEWORKS
BARRIE THOMSON
BEKI POPE
BEN GOVIER
BEN TOPLISS
BEN YOUNG
BIRTHE
BRITA HIRSCH
CAITLIN RYAN
CARMEN DAVAILUS BUCK
CAROLINE DALY
CHARLIE
CHARLIE LOWE
CHELSEA STARNA
CHRIS HART

CHRIS MARSH
CHRISTOFER EDVARDSEN
CINDY ROBB
COLIN & KAREEN CAMPBELL
COLIN MARTIN
COLOURBLIND BOB
CRAIG GREEN
CÉLINE DEBRAY
DAN BELL
DAN DE AROSTEGUI
DANIEL BICKERTON
DARREN BROWN
DAVE POLLITT
DAVE SHENTON
DAVID BEATTIE
DAVID JAYET-LARAFFE
DAVID MOODY
DAVID MORRIS
DAVID MURRAY
DAVID PUGH
DAVID SHAWCROFT
DAVID TAYLOR
DAVID TEW
DAVID WHITEHEAD
DIETER AERTS
DOM O'REILLY
DR JONATHAN RODGERS
ELAINE MCMASTER
ELLIS ORGAN
EMMA EMMENT
EMMA HOMENT
FIONA CHAUTARD
FIONA SHAW
FRASER HAMILTON
FRED ROYLE
GABE
GARETH STACHINI
GARY COOPER
GRAHAM HODGETTS
GREG BAKER
GREY FOX BLOG

GUICHARD JEAN-NICOLAS
GUY PARRY
GUY WIGMORE
HAGEN
HAMLET
HANNAH TOMLINSON
HELEN
HOXTON MINI PRESS
IAN
IAN HOGG
IAN JEFFRIES
IAN TAGGART
J T EVANS
JACK MILLINGTON
JAMES ALMEY
JAMES BORNSHIN
JAMES BRITTAIN
JAMES DAVIES
JAMES HARRIS
JAMES HARVEY
JAMES NORTH
JAMES OCONNELL
JAMES SEDDON
JAMES YOUNG
JANE CROWTHER
JAY JACKSON
JEFFREY WARNOCK
JENNY SHIPLEY
JESS HIGHAM
JO CHRISTOFORIDES
JOE AND STEPHANIE BOSTOCK
JOHANNA KAUPPINEN
JOHN GRAHAN
JOHN LAW
JOHN STEWART
JOHN SUMMERTON
JON MASSEY
JONNY EVANS
KAREN PERCY
KARL RIDLEY
KATE JONES

KATH WHITWORTH
KELDA
KERRY BERRIDGE
KILIAN IDSINGA
KIRSTEN FRANKEL
KOTAATOK
KYLE SOO
LARISSA KUNSTEL-TABET
LAWRENCE GOUGH
LEE ISHERWOOD
LEIF WEISS
LEIGH ANDERSON
LEIGH HIBELL
LEON HEMSLEY
LIZ HOUSE
LLOYD HUGHES
LORENZO DUTTO
LORRAINE AARON
LOUISE FARMAN
LUKE HEATON
LYNDON TURNER
LYNN FRASER
MARCELO E CATARINA
MARIE CARROLL
MARIE FERRER
MARIE SPINKS
MARK BRISTOL
MARK GRADWELL
MARK WEST
MATT MCKINNEY
MATT & BJ HEPWORTH
MATTHEW HOLTON
MATTHEW LEACH
MATTHEW SUFF
MELISSA TENPAA
MICHAEL MENTESSI
MICHAEL WALKER
MIKE JENKINS
MORGAN HAMILTON-GRIFFIN
MR CUP
NATALIE

NATALIE STAPLETON
NEIL COLEMAN
NEIL GREGORY
NEIL MARRA
NICK CHILDS
NICK PETRIE
NICK PLANT
NICKY MOORE
NIKKI SANDERS
OLIVER WILLIAMS
OLLIE APLIN
OMATA
ONE MAN AND HIS MOUSE
OWEN TURNER
PATRICIA VAN DEN AKKER
PAUL BELL
PAUL BURNS
PAUL GOSLING
PAUL MULLEN
PETE THOMAS
PETER SCOTT
PETER SULLIVAN
PETER WILSON
RACHAEL JAMESON
RAOUL LEONARD
REBEKAH MURRAY
RICHARD CLARKE
RICHARD FINLAY
RICHARD SHARP
RIK BARWICK
ROB HALLIFAX
ROBERT FODDERING
ROBERT NEWBOULD
ROBERT THOM
RORY JEFFERS
ROSEMARY JEFFERS
ROSS MACDONALD
RUPERT NEIL BUMFREY
SAM GOATES
SARAH HOLMES
SHAUN

SIMON BANFIELD
SMALL EPIC
SNOWDONIA DISTILLERY
SOPHIE HUCKFIELD
SPENCER ALLEN
STELIOS KALOGREADES
STEPHEN HOLDEN
STEPHEN LEACH
STEVE ARSCOTT
STEVEN PASSANT
STEWART GREENWAY
STUART BLOODWORTH
STUART HOBDAY
TEDDY KEEN
TIM HARRISON
TIM ROYLE
TIM SHARP
TINE MEJER
TOBY HACK
TOM
TOM DALY
TOR WHITE
TRACEY COVE
TRIAS
TROY S
TUERE WIGGINS
TWEEDIE
TYPICA
VANESSA
VICTOR BEATTIE
VICTOR BEUREN
VIVIEN KENWORTHY
WAYNE SHAW
WES ABRAM
WILLIAM AND CLAIRE BUSHELL
XIN DONG
YVONNE AND JOHN ROBERTS
ZOE KERRIGAN

UNTIL NEXT TIME...

—